About CRH

CRH plc was formed in 1970 with the merger of two major Irish companies, Irish Cement and Roadstone, both significant suppliers of building materials to the construction industry in Ireland. Since the merger the Group has become a leading international manufacturer and distributor of building materials, with over 3,700 locations in thirty-five countries worldwide.

CRH is a diversified building materials group which manufactures and distributes building material products, from the fundamentals of heavy materials and elements to construct the frame, through value-added products that complete the building envelope, to distribution channels which service construction fit-out and renewal.

CRH has being doing business in China for a number of years. The Group's primary operations are in northeast China, and in particular in Jilin and Heilongjiang provinces. Through Jilin Yatai Building Materials Company, which is a joint venture with Jilin Yatai Group, CRH is one of the leading producers of cement in China.

Construction accessories (Halfen) and paver products (Sureblock), supplied by CRH subsidiaries in China, have been used in the construction of elements of the Shanghai EXPO.

DOING BUSINESS IN CHINA: THE IRISH EXPERIENCE

爱尔兰企业在中国：跨文化的挑战

LAN LI
CATHAL BRUGHA
LIMING WANG

BLACKHALL
PUBLISHING

Published by Blackhall Publishing
Lonsdale House
Avoca Avenue
Blackrock
Co. Dublin
Ireland

e-mail: info@blackhallpublishing.com
www.blackhallpublishing.com

ISBN: 978-1-84218-207-9

A catalogue record for this book is available from the British Library.

Printed in Shanghai by Shanghai Jiecheng Printing Co. Ltd.

Foreword

Last year saw China celebrating the sixtieth anniversary of the foundation of the modern Chinese state. Being also the thirtieth anniversary of China's official recognition by Ireland, it was an important year for Irish–Chinese relations. China's rapid economic growth and keenness for global trade make it a most exciting place for people looking for new business opportunities.

This year, with the return of China's rapid economic growth and their ongoing keenness for global trade, makes it a most exciting place for Irish businesspeople looking for new opportunities.

This book, the first of its kind, provides an excellent opportunity to learn from the experience of a significantly large and nationwide sample of Irish people with business connections to China. Their testimony of how they have adapted to a business environment that is different and challenging, but also full of energy and opportunity, is filled with insights. Not only those currently engaged in business, but also students and businesspeople of the future, will find much of value within these pages.

In this study we found that Irish people who do business in and with China are enjoying success. Indeed four out of every five respondents to our survey intend to increase their business with China. Irish business-people may have an advantage compared to other foreigners because of similarities between Irish and Chinese culture and history, and because both peoples are very sociable and good at forming human relationships. We would add a note of caution. We have little information about Irish business failure in China. Our research shows that cultural differences are a cause of difficulties for foreigners, and Chinese business practice is embedded within Chinese culture. Almost nine out of every ten respondents thought that information about Chinese business practice was essential for doing business in China, and yet three out of every five of our respondents had not participated in training in culture, language or doing business with China. Success in China involves patience because, within Chinese culture, business relationships are built slowly. Much of our respondents' success seemed to be related to their openness to understanding Chinese business practice and culture. However, even though many Chinese people are becoming fluent in English, it emerged that anyone intending a long-term career in China should learn the Chinese language.

Having done research on and in China for over a decade, and with this research team for over a year, I am struck by how Chinese culture puts a much greater emphasis than we do in Europe on *community*: on family, company, country and especially on social and business networks. My experience of Chinese people is that they are prepared to put a huge and ongoing effort into working for the success of the group; but they will expect you to do the same if you would wish to have a business relationship with them. So, our conclusion is a somewhat sober one: great opportunities for Irish businesses do exist in China, but only for those with the business talent and interest to really contribute, and who are willing to embrace Chinese values regarding community. The same applies to state and other business support agencies: these could be doing more to help businesses to prepare for and then to take advantage of the opportunities.

A well-known example of their community philosophy that we in Ireland could learn from is the Chinese practice of *guanxi* – personal connections – *ceangal* in Irish. So, if you are thinking of doing business in China, or developing your business there, prepare well, and get in touch with at least the following three business support networks: the Ireland China Association, the networks of Irish people working in China and also the networks of Chinese people who are working in Ireland.

Prof. Cathal M. Brugha
Dublin

Preface

At present China is one of the few remaining countries anywhere on the planet that is experiencing growth in its economy, and significant growth at that. In 2009, China's GDP growth was 8.7 per cent and a similar growth is forecast for 2010. China has already overtaken Germany as the world's third largest economy and is well on course to overtake Japan and the US as the world's largest in the not too distant future.

Irish business responded to this unprecedented market opportunity by developing the capabilities to build a successful and fast-expanding trading relationship with China. In 2008, the last year for which full year statistics are available, trade between China and Ireland was worth €7.3 billion; this figure is expected to increase in the next decade.

However, Ireland needs to do more to foster international trade so as to grow its way out of recession and set up a long-run strategy for developing the Irish economy. To this end Ireland needs to focus on increasing opportunities for trade between Ireland and Asia, particularly China. Nevertheless, there is no opportunity without risk. For most Irish companies and organisations China is a distant, culturally different and very fast-changing market. Lack of knowledge of the Chinese market and unique business culture has proven to be a great barrier.

We have for many years been doing research on Irish and Chinese business cultures. This is the first ever major survey of Irish business in China to help Irish businesspeople identify the cultural barriers which prevent them from achieving greater success in the Chinese market.

Compared with previous research in the area, this research is unique in the sense that it provides an empirical study with fresh data collected from Irish businesspeople themselves, and discusses cross-cultural issues in the particular context of the Irish–China business culture. Thus, it is not a general discussion of Chinese business concepts, such as *mianzi* (face), *guanxi* (personal connections) and *renqing* (trading favours), nor is it a case study in which cases of Western business in China are broadly examined. We focus on how Irish businesses deal with the complex and dynamic Chinese market and how Irish businesspeople pick up the intercultural challenge and bridge the cultural barriers in their business dealings in China.

It is in this particular context that we identified the major cultural barriers which Irish business faces in Sino-Irish trade and the relative advantages that Irish businesspeople appear to have when doing business in China. Irish businesspeople do experience cultural shocks in China, as other businesspeople do, such as differences in language, communication and dealings with laws and regulations. However, as a nation that experienced a long period of agrarian society and that suffered from foreign invasion and colonial rule in the past, Ireland shares a certain similarity with China in its cultural traditions; this has differentiated Irish business culture from many others, such as American, German, French and even Japanese culture. Therefore, Ireland should be able to achieve greater success in the Chinese market even though it is geographically and politically distant from China.

In this book, we tell the stories and experiences of Irish businessmen and businesswomen in China, how they learned to adapt to Chinese business practices and how some of the similarities between Irish and Chinese cultures can be a source of business advantage. We believe that such findings will not only benefit Irish businesspeople in exploring their business in Chinese market, but also will contribute to promoting Ireland as a gateway into Europe, an idea generated from the survey research.

From a Chinese perspective, Ireland's success in the Celtic Tiger era was admirably rational and resourceful. Sensibly capitalising on its highly educated workforce and its overseas relationships, Ireland positioned itself very well as an open, attractive and profitable destination for business investment. Its economy became deeply integrated with those of the United States of America and Europe, and, acting as a kind of conduit between these two giants, generated rapid growth for itself. By the same token, however, it was also highly sensitive to reversals in the fortunes of those developed economies on whose business it was reliant. Looking to the future, not only in terms of achieving recovery from the current crisis and its immediate aftermath, but also beyond towards a sustainable longer-term strategy, there are calls for greater engagement by Ireland in the fast-growing economies of the developing world. China was Ireland's tenth largest export market in 2008 and over 100 Irish companies have established entities in China, employing more than 5,000 people.

The enormous potential of doing more business with China offers Ireland two main types of opportunity. In addition to new opportunities for Irish business to trade and profit in China's expanding marketplace where domestic incomes and consumption are rising, China itself is now rapidly 'going global' and investing in other countries.

China's growth pattern has been export-orientated thus far, but the Chinese government has long recognised that this type of economic model is unsustainable as a sole basis for future growth, and has always been aware of the need to plan and implement a restructuring process which will continue to unfold over the coming years as the country heads towards becoming the world's largest economy. There are rational limits to how many Chinese-manufactured goods the rest of the world can consume and, in the wake of the crisis, a fall in demand for Chinese exports hurts employment in the country's manufacturing sector. This has confirmed the intention amongst China's leadership to further develop a different growth mode. Chinese GDP growth has remained high throughout the recent global crisis, bolstered by a huge internal stimulus package. Consequently, despite the setback in export growth rates, China has just overtaken Germany as the world's leading exporting country. At the People's Congress in March 2010, Premier Wen Jiabao returned to the theme of adjustment of China's economic structure and transformation of the economic growth pattern as the focus of the country's current economic policy. Ireland, with its own focus on the 'smart economy', has a clear interest in understanding what China's restructuring could mean for Irish business, as well as meeting the challenge of successfully presenting itself as a gateway into Europe for Chinese multinationals and other investors.

Under this policy of economic restructuring, Chinese domestic expenditure and consumption will increase, which will in turn lead to a rise in imports, meaning more opportunities for foreign companies to sell to China. Premier Wen insists that restructuring is necessary, not only because the economy is too dependent on foreign exports, but also so that incomes can rise and the growing gap between rich and poor can be alleviated. In the last 30 years China has changed completely, from a low income country with an annual GDP per head of around US$300 into a lower-middle income country with an annual GDP per head of around US$3,500. Wen sees disposable incomes continuing to rise and the share of China's ever-growing economic pie more evenly distributed. Increases in government expenditure higher than the predicted 8 per cent GDP growth of

2010 have been planned in areas such as education, healthcare, social security and housing. China's current five-year plan sees the economic development of the country in sustainable balance with the environment. China has set itself ambitious targets for green energy development, environmental protection and lower carbon emissions, as well as turning the economy increasingly towards more hi-tech, innovative and knowledge-based sectors, including new materials industries, bio-industry and the development of financial, distribution and information services. The Economist Intelligence Unit has ranked China as number 1 out of 82 countries in terms of market opportunities between 2010 and 2014.

Turning to China's ODI – outward direct investment – the phenomenal increase in the number of Chinese multinationals emerging onto the world stage over the last decade, from 11 in the Fortune 500 of 2002 to 37 in 2009, is not only further evidence of its transformational development and restructuring economy, but also offers another type of opportunity for Ireland. As these new companies seek further penetration into world markets and investment opportunities overseas, Ireland would benefit greatly by ensuring that its expertise and experience in delivering and catering for the needs of such business is well understood and appreciated in China. This challenge of communication and intercultural dexterity is one for which the adept and resourceful Irish should be well prepared.

Acknowledgements

W e are deeply indebted to the Chinese Language Council International (Hanban) and the Department of Enterprise, Trade and Employment for funding this research project. Special thanks are due to the Embassy of the People's Republic of China in Ireland for cooperating with us in carrying out this research. We also wish to thank University College Dublin (UCD) for its generous support.

We are very much indebted to the Ireland China Association (ICA) for its cooperation and support for the project. We also would like to thank Enterprise Ireland, the Irish Exporters Association, the Asia Forum, the Marketing Institute of Ireland and the Alumni Office of UCD Business School for allowing us to use their databases to send out questionnaires.

We especially wish to express our thanks to the Irish businesspeople who gave up their time to be interviewed, respond to our question-naires and provide information.

We would also like to thank Eileen O'Brien and all at Blackhall Publishing for their work creating this book.

Finally, we are grateful to all of those who worked on the pilot training courses for contributing to the evaluation of this programme.

The UCD Confucius Institute for Ireland
The Irish Institute for Chinese Studies, UCD
For further information please contact China@ucd.ie

Contents

调查结果概述

- 五分之四被调查的爱尔兰公司和机构计划在未来五年里扩展他们在中国的业务。大多数被调查者已经具有三年以上在华经商的经历。

- 几乎所有的被调查者都意识到文化因素对于在华经商成功的重要性。然而，只有不到五分之二的被调查者参加过中国语言、文化以及商务文化方面的培训。

- 被调查者强调爱中两国在商业文化、经营环境以及围绕人际关系的文化问题方面存在着重要差异。84.3%的被调查者指出良好的人际关系是在中国市场取得进一步成功的关键；88%的人指出了解有关中国商务的信息至关重要。

- 67.8%的被调查者认为，了解中国市场是取得在华经商成功的三个重要的社会文化因素之一。在这方面，了解与中国市场相关的方针政策、规章制度、法律体系以及商法被认为是对爱尔兰公司和机构的一个严峻挑战。在应对中国的规章制度和政府的各项政策方面，超过五分之二和近三分之一的被调查者分别表示了关注。

- 一些被调查者认为比起其它欧洲国家和美国的商人，爱尔兰商人因爱中两国某些文化和历史的相似之处，更容易融入中国市场。近半数的被调查者认为，与其它欧洲国家或美国文化相比，爱尔兰文化与中国文化之间有更多的相似点。为数不少的被调查者认为在涉及人际关系的四个方面爱中文化之间有相近之处，其中 56.8%的被调查者认为两国的商务文化都强调依赖人际关系做生意；48.2%认为两国商人都十分重视利用长期合作建立双方的信任；46.8% 认为建立相互之间的友谊在两国商务交往中受到共同的重视；45.9%认为两国商人都非常尊重家庭价值。

- 尽力克服文化差异的障碍是取得在华经商成功的关键。53.6%的被调查者认为爱尔兰文化与中国文化"鲜有相似"的主要方面是"注重给面子和避免丢面子"；36.1%认为是"尊重和服从权威"；34.3% 认为是"灵活机动地运用规章制度"。

- 建立爱中商业人士之间的信任被认为需要付出长期的、多方面的努力。考虑到中国政治、社会和经济体系的不同，61.4%的被调查者认为对跨文化知识的掌握以及对这一知识重要性的认识是建立双方之间信任的关键。半数以上的被调查者认为职场能力、兑现承诺、语言能力和人际关系也对建立这一信任至关重要。

- 半数以上的被调查者认为畅通的信息渠道是在中国经商的另一个必不可少的条件。然而，超过半数的爱尔兰公司和机构在中国尚未设立办事机构。他们承认缺少必要的信息阻碍了他们在华取得更大的成功。

- 在中国已经设立了办事机构的被调查者更清醒地意识到人际关系在中国商业环境中的重要性。他们之中 93%的人认为"良好的人际关系"已经或者必将促进对华商贸业务的成功。而在尚未设立驻中国办事机构的公司和机构中持有这一观点的被调查者只有 75%。

- 爱中两国之间贸易的快速增长也增强了对中国语言、文化以及商务短期培训的需求。被调查者对培训的形式和内容各有不同的侧重与选取。其中对短期强化班感兴趣的占 52%，晚间课程班 40.2%，中国语言和文化在职学位班 27.5%，中国学习之旅 25.5%，在线远程学习 24.5%，侧重中国商学的工商管理硕士夏令营班 21.6%。

- 调查结果显示，爱尔兰的公司和机构对具有中国语言、文化、社会以及商务背景的商学毕业生有很高的需求。例如，78.4%和 48.5%返回调查问卷的爱尔兰公司和机构分别对具有上述背景的商学本科毕业生和硕士毕业生感兴趣。对其它专业毕业生感兴趣的数据分别为：16.5%中国学本科毕业生，14.4%当代中国研究硕士毕业生，12.4%民法与中国学本科毕业生，10.3%政治与中国学本科毕业生。

About the Authors

RESEARCH TEAM LEADER: LAN LI, PHD

Lecturer, Irish Institute for Chinese Studies, UCD

Dr Lan Li received her BA and MA in Chinese Language and Literature at Renmin University, Beijing. She then took up a lectureship position at the university, lecturing on the History and Theory of Ancient Chinese Literature. In 1991 she received a scholarship from Queen's University Belfast for her PhD in Social Anthropology, which was also funded by the Royal Anthropological Institute of Great Britain and Ireland. Her doctoral thesis, entitled 'Nuo: Shamanism among the Tujia of Southwest China', studied the rise of popular religions in contemporary China and was later published in book form. Dr Li is a member of the British Association for Chinese Studies and the Association for Chinese Studies in Ireland. She lectured in Chinese language, culture and modern Chinese society at Queen's University Belfast until 2006. In September 2006, Dr Li joined the Irish Institute for Chinese Studies in UCD as a lecturer in Chinese Studies. Her research interest is in the beliefs of Chinese people in contemporary China, intercultural issues between China and Ireland and the status of Chinese migrant workers in Ireland. Dr Li can be contacted by email at lan.li@ucd.ie.

RESEARCH TEAM LEADER: CATHAL BRUGHA, PHD, MBA, MSC, FMII

Director, Centre for Business Analytics, School of Business, UCD

Professor Cathal M. Brugha (http://mis.ucd.ie/staff/cbrugha) is the director of the Centre for Business Analytics in the School of Business, University College Dublin. He has a BSc and MSc in Mathematical Science from UCD, an MBA from TCD, and a PhD in Combinatorial Optimisation from UCD. After a career in DIT he joined UCD in 1991.

As President of the Management Science Society of Ireland since 1992 he has represented Ireland annually at council meetings of the European Association of Operational Research Societies (EURO) and the International Federation of Operational Research Societies (IFORS). He was editor of the IFORS journal, *International Transactions in Operational Research*, from 2000 to 2006.

He is a Fellow of the Marketing Institute of Ireland, and was for many years chair/member of the Institute's education committee, and an external examiner.

His main theoretical research is in Nomology, the study of the decision processes of the mind, the structures or 'covering laws' that frame people's thinking and provide commonalities between different fields and cultures. He is currently testing these structures through empirical surveys of business relationships and intercultural trust between China and Ireland. His applied work is focused on generic decision methodologies and on multi-criteria measurement (see www.mcdm.com).

He has been a Visiting Professor at the China Academy of Science in Beijing in 2006 and Xidian University, Xi'an in 2009.

He has been a member of several international editorial boards, including the *European Journal of Operational Research* (1994–2007) and, as a founder member, the *International Journal of Knowledge and Systems Sciences* (2004–date), and a reviewer for many others.

PRINCIPAL INVESTIGATOR: LIMING WANG, PHD

Director, Irish Institute for Chinese Studies at UCD, UCD Confucius Institute for Ireland

Born and brought up in China, Dr Wang worked for six and a half years (as a Deputy Division Director from 1986) for the Ministry of Commerce of the People's Republic of China in Beijing following his primary degree, obtained in 1982. In 1989, he completed an International MBA course in Sheffield Hallam University as a visiting student. He was subsequently awarded a visiting studentship from Queen's University Belfast and, after completing his PhD in Economics, became a teaching and research fellow at Queen's in 1995. From 2000, he worked as a Senior Research Fellow and Head of the China Unit, which is primarily involved in managing the expansion and development of Queen's links with China in teaching, research and joint programmes.

Dr Wang was appointed at the beginning of 2006 to establish and run the Irish Institute for Chinese Studies at UCD. He was also appointed as the director of the UCD Confucius Institute for Ireland.

Outside of UCD, Dr Wang is the Chairman of the Association for Chinese Studies in Ireland, the Secretary General of the Chinese Economic Association in Europe and a Board Director of the Institute of International Trade of Ireland. He has been a Visiting Professor at Huazhong University of Science and Technology (2002–2004) and Anhui Normal University since 2003. He has also been a member of the international editorial board for the *Journal of Chinese Economic and Business Studies* since 2003.

RESEARCH TEAM MEMBERS

In alphabetical order

Mr Eoin Brugha
School of Computer Science and Informatics, UCD

Prof. Rong Du
School of Economics and Management, Xidian University, China

Ms Zhe Fang
Nottingham Trent University, formerly of Gallup China

Ms Xia Han
Smurfit School of Business, UCD

Mr Zengyu Huang
Smurfit School of Business, UCD

Mr Francis Kane
Irish Institute for Chinese Studies, UCD

Ms Helen Mahony
Consultant on Chinese Business Affairs, Dublin

Mr Wei Zhang
UCD Confucius Institute for Ireland

Introduction

Irish Business in China: Meeting the Intercultural Challenges

It used to be traditional in the West to talk about the 'mysteries of the Orient'. We rarely hear this nowadays, possibly because information communications technology (ICT) has given us the impression of a shrinking planet, that anything is possible and everything is visible. Our experience, as authors of this book on the first ever major survey of Irish business in China, is that we would wish to dispel the notion that intercultural business relationships are easy, while affirming that there are great opportunities for Irish business with China.

Building business with Chinese people, and in China, is a multi-layered activity. In this chapter we would like to give an idea of the extent and depth of these layers. Throughout the book we give illustrations from our interviews with Irish businesspeople of how they dealt with the difficulties they encountered. A lot is already known. If we are to add anything it would be to confirm what is generally understood, but then emphasise that what has to be done to achieve success is not a question of overcoming barriers, but more about understanding and addressing real cultural differences. Also, with China, building business relationships is never short term, always long term. So, 'if you fail to plan, you plan to fail'.

A certain amount of business can be done over the internet, Skype and phone, and through using connections, especially where there is obvious advantage to both sides. But, generally, if you want to do business in China you have to go there, and get to know the Chinese people.

The next layer relates to politeness and good manners. Chinese people respect importance, size and power, and a businessperson on his or her first engagement with Chinese business will learn the little things, such as how to give and receive business cards, how to listen rather than speak first at business meetings and how to respect the rank and position of people on the other side. If you are not able to adjust your ways of interacting socially to take account of Chinese culture, don't bother coming to China!

Your first venture into the unknown will be when you get to hear about *guanxi* (personal connections) and possibly *mianzi* (face). There are several dangers here. The fact that these culturally distinctive Chinese ways are named tends to give artificial comfort, that naming means explaining. In fact it is the opposite. The reason they are named is precisely because they are so hard to explain in terms of Western culture, which is because Chinese culture comes from a 'different place', to which it may take you a long time to adjust. The other danger is thinking that you can rely on what is written about *guanxi* and *mianzi*, including what is written by academics. First of all, if it is difficult for Westerners to understand Easterners, it is also difficult for Easterners to understand Westerners, possibly even more so. Consequently, it is difficult for Chinese people to explain what *guanxi* and *mianzi* mean in terms that Westerners can understand. Secondly, we believe that much of the understanding of *guanxi* and *mianzi* can come only from empirical research such as this, a research of Chinese business culture based on a survey of Irish business-people. In Ireland, the people who really understand these things are the businesspeople who have been involved in business dealings with China for a certain period of time. Usually they are too busy to write books and articles. And also they don't see why they should tell others about them, and throw away their competitive advantage. Thirdly, we, the authors, are two Chinese and a European who have been working together for years. We see many similarities between China and Ireland, which we will discuss later. We see America as more different. Yet many of the East–West intercultural studies that have been reported were done in America or some European countries such as Germany, France and the UK, or involved Chinese scholars whose experience of the West was in America or in the European countries mentioned above. Not only may they be incorrect, but what they say may not apply to relationships between some European countries like Ireland and China.

Next in this multi-layered exploration is to try from your Western viewpoint to understand Chinese concerns and interests. A way to begin is to try to understand their history, culture, societal customs and ways of relating. And a way to start this is to *learn* some of these, including some simple Chinese greetings. The Chinese people are socially hospitable, friendly and polite. So, even some initial interactions will give you a few glimpses of how they are different. Furthermore, because their past experience of Westerners, historically, culturally and (often) personally, has not been great, they will be delighted and surprised if you make a decent effort to relate to them.

From here we will describe some of these differences. They are like nuances, or style preferences. In general, Westerners, before they decide to do business, tend to wish to *convince* themselves that their Chinese partners have the capabilities to deliver, and that they are capable of benefitting from, or meeting the expectations of, the relationship. Westerners are more concerned with being *convinced* first, and then with building *relationship communities*.

The Chinese tend to prefer to build *communities* and *relationships* first. This applies to building both long-term and short-term relationships. A Western person might expect results from the first visit to China as proof that it is a good idea. A Chinese person will see a first visit as 'getting to know you', possibly with a view to a ten- or twenty-year relationship. Social meetings, discussions and evening meals are essential to Chinese relationship-building. Even for short-term, smaller interactions, Chinese people will feel it is rude and disrespectful to do business before socially interacting. They will prefer to first re-establish the relationship. They are more concerned with building *relationship communities* first, and then with being *convinced* within the relationship that it is possible to do business. They are looking for a feeling of mutual comfort before proceeding.

A key test for Chinese people to convince them that this process of community building is succeeding is *reciprocity*. They will take initiatives such as giving invitations to meet, to have a meal, to visit them in their home, all of which have very particular meaning and social status. Part of this is to get an opportunity to know the other person. But, also, they are looking for clues to the seriousness of the intent of their prospective partner, and more. How quick are the Westerners to 'catching on' to what they have in mind? How capable are they of building the relationship? How likely is it that they will make this relationship productive? For Westerners generous invitations to a meal or to visit a Chinese family in their home can be baffling, because they would not be likely to do the same. This bafflement can lead them to 'park' this activity, and file it under 'things that Chinese people do that I don't understand'; whereas it actually is an invitation to strengthen the relationship. Failure to reciprocate is equivalent to showing a disinclination to do what is necessary to build a business relationship.

This interaction between these two activities of 'community building' and 'convincing' differentiates Europeans and the Chinese from one another, but differentiates both from Americans, who are more concerned with their own commitments, resources, points of view and interests, and less with where their business partners may be. We should be careful here, because generalisations are dangerous, and there are different types of Americans; those who travel abroad tend to be in the group that is more open to cultural difference. However, Americans tend to be slower to 'invest' in entertainment before they 'have a deal'.

There are also differences amongst European cultures. Because Chinese people appear to be 'inscrutable', although this is truer of Japanese culture, it would be wrong to think that they are not 'warm'. So, some people coming from Nordic/Anglo-Saxon/Germanic cultures may not get on so well with Chinese people. Chinese people tend to be restrained, especially in the initial formation of relationships. Consequently, some of the Latin countries can have difficulties.

Irish people have some starting advantages in relationships with Chinese people. For a start, both like to socialise, to talk, especially about family, and to do all of these combined with food – and drink. Both also have a history of oppression by empires, and also by central government. For Ireland this is not just about its treatment over seven centuries by the British Empire. Listen to the tone when someone from Cork talks about the 'Dublin government' or someone from Mayo says 'it's all very well for ye up in Dublin'. In Ireland many people go to their local politicians to get something that is their entitlement. This embeddedness of politics in the community is close in some ways to that of the Communist Party in China, although not as formalised.

One enormous difference is about hierarchy and levels. In Ireland most people feel that they could be on first-name terms with someone who is on first-name terms with a senior politician, and would not be surprised if they met one of the most powerful people in Ireland next weekend. In China, not only is the hierarchical ladder very high, but when they meet in a group, which is often, they are highly aware of the 'pecking order' in the group. Furthermore, ranks and titles mean a lot, and are used in meetings, especially formal meetings. You must be aware of the status of each person in the group that you will meet, and of your own group. If you are the leader, you will be expected to take a leader's role, to introduce the rest of the group and speak on its behalf, and to represent your group to the leader of the Chinese group, including in formal summaries of the business activities. Not to do so could be seen as an insult, and an indication of intention about the business relationship.

Next is the issue of learning the Chinese language. In the business world most Chinese people have very good English, certainly good enough to transact business relationships. If your intent is to do business for a few years you don't need to learn Chinese. But not trying to learn it, when you have spent five years in China, or you are expressing the intent to build a twenty-year relationship, will create a social barrier between you and the Chinese that will lead to difficulties with building personal connections, which are key to doing business in China. This leads to a great difference between East and West regarding trust. For Westerners trust is highly inter-personal, and is an emotional feeling about how a relationship will 'stand up' in a situation. A Westerner will make a judgement about another's character, that the other is 'trustworthy', that their value systems are such that they are deemed to be ethical, honest, reliable and true to their word. They might even make this 'call' after a brief meeting with another person. If they employ a Chinese person they could not conceive that their employee could deceive them, because in the West this could 'ruin a person's reputation'.

Again this is the difference between the priorities; between the European 'convincing' and the Chinese 'community' focus. When someone breaks trust with a Westerner he or she will be 'very disappointed'. They will say 'I was convinced that he/she was a good person. I cannot understand why he/she let me down. I don't know how I could have made such a poor judgement.'

In China a person will be part of many communities, serving the interests of family, friends, business relationships – of many different types. Legal contracts, between business entities, or between employers and employees, are frequently impossible to implement. Company ownership can change overnight. Trust in this context is more about the strength of competing bonds, and the consequences of serving the interests of one group more than another. This can go in two ways. On the one hand a Chinese person can build a bond virtually 'for life' with another, including a Westerner, and will be prepared to share their 'future' with the other. It is very important for a Westerner to recognise the signals when this is possible. Such relationships can be very fulfilling and rewarding in many ways, not just from a business point of view; they can lead to lifelong friendships. On the other hand, if a Chinese person thinks that a relationship is weak or unimportant to them they may have no compunction about misleading the other person in the relationship. Relationships with strangers, known as '*sheng-ren*', is a very weak bond. This can be confusing to a Westerner, as it appears to imply a lack of ethics. First of all, within Chinese culture, the decision to commit to a relationship, and the nature of that commitment, comes much later, after the relationship has been formed. Secondly, within the Chinese hierarchical system only the top person has the authority to make a promise on behalf of the institution, which makes every 'promise' a conditional statement of intent, but also every contract subject to possible change by another authority.

The other side of this coin is that Chinese people can find Western organisations confusing. Chinese people will expect that the head of an organisation to be in charge, and to dictate policy for the organisation. So, a deal made with the head of an organisation is a deal done. They will find it hard to understand that a Western organisation can be a loose federation of numerous empires, each with their own authority over their own section. That does not mean that there is stability and consistency on the Chinese side. The fluidity in Chinese organisations, the lack of a culture of legal contracts, and the sense that relationships are between and within communities of people, means that business arrangements are frequently modified and adjusted, re-interpreted and refined as circumstances change. The Chinese way to offset this is by continuous communication and discussion.

The Chinese view of trust is closer to what happens in the 'Prisoners' Dilemma' game. Two friends are accused of the same crime. The authorities offer both an incentive to blame the other. Do they cooperate with the authorities, or do they remain loyal to their friend? And what do they think their friend is likely to do? The dilemma is that they have to find a balance between respect for the authorities and their relationship.

The Irish businesspeople we interviewed as part of this research were in most cases individual entrepreneurs; they might be better described as pioneers. Only recently have larger Irish companies begun to figure considerably, such as CRH and Treasury Holdings. Consequently, the amount of business between China and Ireland has been small compared to what it could be. How might it grow considerably? We offer here a radical suggestion, that Ireland become China's gateway into Europe. Ireland helped the United States with its internationalisation into Europe over the past half-century. It could do so for China over the next fifty years, but in a different way. China's relationships with the West have been focused on getting access to technology and resources. China is becoming the globe's major trading region, and the major producer of many high quality, reasonably priced goods, such as textiles. As the standard of living in China is rising other Asian countries are competing to produce at a lower price. Chinese exporters cannot afford to continue indefinitely to be 'price-takers' internationally, and to not be able to influence the 'conditions of sale' of their products in the West.

Ireland could offer such a relationship to China, facilitating entry of Chinese products into Europe, through the formation of joint-venture supply chain companies. The emphasis would be on facilitation and relationship building. To make it work would require the enthusiastic participation of the community of Irish people who have built business in China, and then of the Irish government itself, as well as its agencies, and a long-term commitment to such a *guanxi* relationship.

In our opinion such a relationship is possible between the Irish and the Chinese, and easier to do than with many other countries.

Chapter 1

Background to the Research

BACKGROUND BRIEFING

China's rapid and sustainable economic growth has propelled it to become the world's third largest economy today and potentially the largest in the foreseeable future. This development has seen China's 1.3 billion people begin a process of integration into the global economy and become a major driving force in the process of globalisation, particularly since joining the World Trade Organization in 2001.

China is often regarded as the most influential emerging economy due to the size and scale of its successes over the last three decades. More importantly, in the current economic crisis, China appears to be the first large economy to begin the recovery process, and is likely to be the first to converge back towards its long-term potential growth path with a more balanced and sustainable pattern.

Ireland and China's excellent relations have blossomed significantly over the past two decades. Ireland, one of the smaller countries of the world in size and population, has, in recent years, developed the capability to build a successful and fast-expanding trading relationship with the world's largest market. However, it is also true that in comparison with other developed nations, Irish companies and organisations have been relatively slow in taking advantage of the opportunities available to foreign business in China. One of the major problems is that culturally most Irish companies and organisations are not ready or properly prepared to enter the Chinese market. They have not fully appreciated the importance of awareness and understanding of the Chinese language and Chinese culture and business practice, nor have they received proper training in the knowledge and skills required before starting doing business in or with China.

As part of their work to help Irish businesses to bridge the gap, the newly established UCD Confucius Institute for Ireland and Irish Institute for Chinese Studies initiated this nationwide survey of firms and companies in Ireland on the needs for support, including expertise in Chinese business and training in the Chinese language and Chinese culture and business practices.

PREVIOUS SURVEYS AND RESEARCH ON IRISH BUSINESS IN CHINA

A key issue in international business is how to cope with the highly distinctive institutional and cultural environments of the host country.[1] As a consequence of its policy of market liberalisation in the past few decades, China has become a 'star performer' in terms of its economic growth and a lucrative market for foreign investment. There has been a flurry of business ventures between domestic Chinese firms and foreign entities, which run the spectrum from complex joint ventures and cross-border mergers to a variety of exporting and outsourcing arrangements.[2]

There is no doubt that China has moved dramatically towards a more market-oriented economy; the Chinese market, however, remains very different from the West. There are several challenges that confront foreign firms operating in China. First is the uniqueness of the Chinese socialist market economy; second, the underdevelopment of the social infrastructure; and third, the dominance of traditional Chinese culture in business activities.[3] For these reasons, Western companies often find that it is difficult to obtain information about potential orders in China, and about what is the appropriate way to influence Chinese decision-makers so as to win business deals.

Business ventures in China are often characterised by friction, failure and financial loss. Some of the most common problems that have been encountered by European firms conducting business in China have been identified by researchers.[4] The most commonly cited difficulties are the barriers to effective communication that arise through differences of language and culture. The second issue when trading in China is the lack of knowledge and information about the market. Thirdly, the difficulty experienced in recruiting local staff of a suitable quality is another problem that often arises. Last but not least is the lack of understanding about the complicated regulations for different industries and the protection of intellectual property rights in China, which remains weak compared to Western countries.

So far, however, limited research has been done to address the cultural issues that Irish people might encounter in China, whether as academic scholars or business organisations. To date, only Enterprise Ireland provides a guide for Irish companies about doing business in China.[5]

In the 1990s, a survey conducted on Irish and UK language training providers for businesses found extremely low levels of companies performing target country business culture audits or requesting information on business culture or training from providers of target country language training.[6] Nearly all providers, 88.4 per cent, reported that 0–25 per cent of companies had performed target country culture audits and 72 per cent said that 0–25 per cent requested cultural information and training alongside language training. Given that cultural fluency can mean the difference between success and failure in business, the implications were clear at that time for both training providers and companies. Great potential for the development of appropriate training courses in cultural fluency was demonstrated, as was the huge gap in companies proactively seeking such training. Researchers Randelsome and Myers posited that for the sake of competitive advantage in business, language fluency may be desirable, but cultural fluency is 'downright indispensable'.[7]

An examination of Chinese-related Masters theses for the years 2002 to 2008 in the UCD Smurfit School of Business found that some empirical research has already been conducted in relation to the cultural issues facing Irish companies and organisations doing business with China. At the macro level, Taylor and Trampedach made comprehensive descriptions of the Chinese market; however, these descriptions did not consider the cultural issues from a uniquely Irish business perspective.[8] Interestingly, Trampedach noted that smaller companies are more likely to succeed in China, but did not substantiate his finding with any evidence.[9]

Given the competitive advantages that Irish firms enjoy in terms of research and innovation, Li focused on the entry strategies of Irish information technology (IT) firms into the Chinese market.[10] He found that although Irish firms are quite experienced regarding foreign market entry in general, they appear to know very little about the Chinese market or the country's changing landscape of laws and regulations. Furthermore, the language and cultural differences present another challenge for Irish companies trying to gain access to this greater customer base. In addition, Irish firms are often small in size, which may make it difficult for them to recruit and retain skilled people so as to compete with other multinationals in China.

It is not uncommon to hear of complaints from both Irish and Chinese companies at the negotiation stage. Corless carried out in-depth interviews with four Irish businessmen about intercultural negotiations with Chinese partners.[11] She identified that the motivations for them to set up operations in China are cost reduction, market expansion and development of new products. The interviews embraced a wide range of topics which are of key concern for Irish companies when negotiating with their Chinese counterparts, such as business etiquette, different stages of negotiations, and strategies and tactics used in negotiations. However, she did not take into account other cultural issues, such as the importance of face (*mianzi*) and the management of social relations (*guanxi*) within the Chinese context.

Knowing that establishing business in China is a complicated task, in his report on the challenges to the successful implementation of Irish projects in China, Keane conducted semi-structured interviews with five individuals who not only have a good understanding of both countries' cultures, but also have first-hand experience with Irish projects in the Chinese market.[12] He found that the establishment of trust is a huge issue for both Irish and Chinese employees to work as a team. Another problem is miscommunication, which is mainly caused by the language barrier. He proposed that finding a competent interpreter could help Irish businesspeople overcome the language barrier and reduce the risk of misunderstanding.

Additionally, Keane observed that an ability to speak some Mandarin, even a few words, can demonstrate long-term intentions, while showing respect for Chinese culture and helping to build up mutual trust between Irish businesspeople and their Chinese partners. O'Broin and McQuillan recognised the fact that although there is a wealth of literature about Sino-American business, there is a corresponding dearth on the European side, and even fewer accessible papers pertaining to Ireland's specific business transactions with China.[13] To this end, they compared and contrasted the business cultures of the two through Hofstede's five cultural indicators.* The conclusions they reached tend to conform to the popular

---

* Hofstede's work on cultural dimensions in business is widely referred to. He measures different organisational cultures in terms of the national cultures to which they belong and devised the following indicators: 1. Low vs. High Power Distance, 2. Individualism vs. Collectivism, 3. Masculinity vs. Femininity, and 4. Low vs. High Uncertainty Avoidance. Hofstede has recently included a fifth indicator: Long-term Orientation vs. Short-term Orientation.

belief that the Irish management style in general mirrors that of American organisations. They advocated the perception that in Ireland, as in the US, management is characterised by low power distance, with managers forming work relationships on an informal basis, whereas the Chinese management style is traditionally 'paternalistic', as control is centralised and authority is reinforced through a hierarchical power structure within the company.

After several semi-structured interviews with respondents who have extensive experience in Irish–Chinese transactions, O'Broin and McQuillan took the view that in order to build a sound relationship with a Chinese partner, it is necessary for Irish firms to educate their own organisations about Chinese business culture and etiquette. Furthermore, managers must enrol themselves and their staff directly in Chinese culture and business seminars. Last but not least, the establishment of 'guanxi' was often considered by respondents as time-consuming. Therefore, they suggested that companies find a Chinese consultancy firm to act as an intermediary, which would help in negotiations and provide a network of contacts.

Using a quantitative study with 50 respondents, mostly from Irish firms, Goggin identified the critical factors that prevented Western businesses from achieving greater success in the Chinese market.[14] These included bureaucracy, a hierarchical social structure, the paternalistic management style and, in particular, the difficulties with establishing a 'guanxi' network. She found that the Irish businesspeople surveyed had problems in building up trust and 'ganqing' relationships (based on affection or empathy) with their Chinese partners and it was difficult for them to understand the concepts of 'renqing' (obligations) and 'mianzi' (face), which derive from the cultural tradition of Confucianism. She argued that the establishment of an effective 'guanxi' network was one of the critical concerns of many Irish firms.

Chapter 2

Objectives of the Survey Research

Designed as a national survey of Irish companies and organisations that have been doing or intend to do business in or with China, the objectives of the research were as follows:

1. To identify the cultural factors which have helped Irish companies and organisations achieve success in doing business in or with China, or which have prevented them from achieving success
2. To assess the demand of Irish companies and organisations for support and expertise in Chinese business and training in Chinese language and culture
3. To provide the Irish Institute for Chinese Studies in UCD and the UCD Confucius Institute for Ireland with appropriate information towards the design of degree programmes that involve Chinese Studies, and training programmes in Chinese language and culture to meet the needs of Irish companies and organisations
4. To provide the Irish government with information about the cultural barriers Irish firms are confronting when conducting business in China, and recommend approaches that would facilitate Irish higher education to keep pace with the new demands of Irish business in today's rapidly changing world

Chapter 3

Participants in the Survey

Survey participants were people with experience of China through their work in Irish companies, government agencies or the education sector.

QUESTIONNAIRE SURVEY PARTICIPANTS

In total, 117 returned questionnaires were received from survey respondents.

Among the people who responded to our questionnaire survey, 93.1 per cent were Irish and 79.5 per cent male; 27.4 per cent were in the age group of 25–35 years old, 28.2 per cent 35–45 years, 24.8 per cent 45–55 years and 17.9 per cent over 55 years of age.

Regarding position within the company, 67.5 per cent of the participants were owners/directors/senior management, 16.2 per cent middle management and 11.1 per cent junior management/executive.

The service and education sector comprised 57.3 per cent of respondents, 20.8 per cent were in manufacturing, 16.7 per cent in export/import, and the remainder in marketing/retail.

Regarding company size, 25 per cent of respondents employed less than 10 people, 41.4 per cent employed between 10 and 150 people, and 33.6 per cent employed more than 150 people.

Over one-fifth, 21.7 per cent, of respondents claimed that over 35 per cent of their revenue was based on the Chinese market, 40.9 per cent claimed 1–10 per cent, and 37.4 per cent claimed less than 1 per cent.

Over the past three years, 70.4 per cent of the business settings employed Chinese employees: 54.3 per cent for a period of more than three years, 37 per cent for one to three years, and 8.6 per cent for less than one year.

Questioned on whether they had a physical presence in China, 50.4 per cent of respondents did, while 68.4 per cent had a business partner and/or representative in China.

The survey also found that 72.8 per cent had been doing business in or with China for more than three years, 16.7 per cent for a period of one to three years, 4.4 per cent for less than twelve months, and 6.1 per cent had never done business with China.

INTERVIEW SURVEY PARTICIPANTS

Brief profiles of the people who participated in our interview survey are given in Table 1.

Table 1:   Interviewee Profiles

Profession/Position	Category
Director	Education
Partner	Legal
Chief correspondent	Media
Council member	Media
China director	Government agency
Founder	Import/export
President	Business network organisation
Principal scientist	Electronics/Fortune global 500
Partner	Consulting/accounting/Fortune global 500
Consultant	Consulting/engineering
Chief representative	Government agency
Serial entrepreneur	Real estate/investment
Manager	Telecom/ICT/Fortune global 500
Owner	Import/export
Consultant	Consulting service
Lawyer	Law firm
Owner	Manufacturing/importing
Project coordinator	Education
International officer	Education
Engineer	Global telecommunications company
Owner/director	Large merchandising company
Manager	Finance
Owner	Service industry in China
Middle management	Consultancy company
Employee	Chinese education agency
Manager	Finance
Civil servant	Irish embassy in China
Middle management	Manufacturing

Chapter 4

Main Findings

In this chapter, the main findings of the survey research will be provided and various cultural issues in relation to doing business in China will be discussed. Firstly, the factors which have contributed or will contribute to business success in China are examined, such as good personal relationships, cultural knowledge, understanding institutional aspects of the Chinese market, communication skills, access to information sources and language ability. Although the cultural factors have been commonly discussed among business circles and in the academic world, the findings are interesting and unique in the sense that they are the stories told by businesspeople themselves, who may not necessarily share the stories with others if they did not participate in the survey research we carried out. The discussion is followed by a special section to examine similarities and differences between Irish and Chinese business cultures, which is one of the key issues identified in the survey research and has been recognised as crucial in achieving greater success in the Chinese market. The importance of the discussion lays in the fact that both Irish businesspeople and those from other cultural backgrounds may find it beneficial to know what similarities one's own culture shares with others since such knowledge can help businesspeople make good use of cultural closeness to build personal relationships with their business partners in other countries and adapt to a strange business environment easily and quickly. In the third section the issue of intercultural trust in the particular context of Chinese business culture will be examined and factors that contribute to building successful mutual trust will be discussed. In the last section, problems preventing businesspeople achieving greater success in China are identified, such as the language barrier, issues with Chinese regulations, miscommunication, difficulties with mutual trust, information scarcity and lack of personal connections.

When asked about their business involvement in China over the next five years, 79.3 per cent of respondents planned to increase their business with China over the period, 9.5 per cent to start doing business in China, 6.8 per cent to remain unchanged, and the remaining 5.2 per cent were evenly divided in their plans to decrease or stop doing business with China within five years (see Chart 1).

The vast majority of Irish businesspeople surveyed had experience of doing business in China: 83 respondents out of 117 (72.8 per cent) had more than three years' experience, nineteen (16.7 per cent) more than twelve months' but less than three years', and five (4.4 per cent) less than twelve months' experience (see Chart 2). The high percentage of respondents with more than three years' experience of doing business in China is significant to analysis of the survey data. Long-term business involvement with China gives Irish businesspeople the time to experience and understand the importance of cultural awareness for their business success in the Chinese business environment. Thus, 113 respondents out of 117 (96.6 per cent) responded positively to the following question: 'In your opinion, how important is an awareness of cultural factors for a company to have success in dealing with Chinese companies?' Eighty-six out of 117 (73.5 per cent) responded 'very important' and 27 (23.1 per cent) 'important' (see Chart 3).

FACTORS WHICH HAVE CONTRIBUTED OR WILL CONTRIBUTE TO BUSINESS SUCCESS IN CHINA

More than half of the respondents viewed the following five factors as having contributed or going to contribute to their business success in China:

- Good personal relationships
- Cultural knowledge
- Understanding of the Chinese market
- Communication skills
- Access to information sources

Around 40 per cent of respondents identified four further factors:

- Competent interpreters
- Language ability

- Sufficient information
- Help from the Irish government

The remaining three factors, considered important by less than 40 per cent of respondents, were:

- Expertise in Chinese business
- The Chinese government's policies
- The Irish government's policies

See Chart 4.

Good Personal Relationships

Of the factors which the Irish businesspeople surveyed thought have contributed or will contribute to their business success in China, 'good personal relationship' was ranked top, with 97 respondents out of 117 (84.3 per cent) indicating it. In the interviews, a frequent comment was that while personal relationships are important in all business, they are to a far greater extent important when doing business in China (see Chart 4). The better businesspeople know China, the more they appear to appreciate how essential human relations are in the Chinese business environment. Of the survey participants who had a physical presence in China, as many as 93 per cent indicated that 'good personal relationships' have contributed or will contribute to their business success, compared with 75 per cent of those with no physical presence (see Chart 5).

Awareness of Different Sociocultural Concepts

Irish businesspeople are generally aware of the different sociocultural backgrounds that differentiate the way the Irish do business from that of the Chinese. Compared with Western business culture, the Chinese emphasis is on human relations – a core concept of Chinese cultural tradition, which has been significantly influenced by Confucianism. The interview respondents were very vocal on these differences, and eager to share what they had learned from their experiences of doing business with Chinese people:

> Everything here [in China] is based on 'who-knows-who', which is opposite to the Western concept of 'who-knows-what'. (F1)

> In Western companies, time is money, time is money, time is money; for Chinese companies, time is investment in relation-ships. (H5)

> [In China] business isn't simply, 'You want that, so I'll sell it to you for a dollar.' To them [Chinese businesspeople], business is more relationship-based and so they have to like you. They must like the product but then they have to like you as well and they have to think, 'Am I happy to do business with this guy now and also in the future?' (CL15)

Irish businesspeople's understanding of the differences in customs and social behaviour has helped them to realise the importance of building personal relationships in their business dealings with China:

> The business meetings are quite important but they are not the main forum for conducting the business, the main forum is the business dinners that are conducted after. (F2)

> I think this is just an accepted part of business in China, taking people out for dinner, giving them gifts, giving them perks; I think that is the way things are done over there. (H3)

> You really need to get down on the ground, you need to spend time with them, you need to go out incessantly, eating with them, dining with them, trying to learn as much as possible about the little social idiosyncrasies which you must respect and acknowledge and adhere to when you are socialising with them. They are only small things but they mean a lot. (H5)

> Some of the times I go to China, it is not for a specific piece of business, it's just to catch up with people, and that is necessary. (H2)

Relationships Contribute to Business Success in China

In our survey, four specific relationships were identified by Irish businesspeople as having helped them achieve business success in China: with government officials, with business partners, being part of an intercultural marriage/partnership, and with the Chinese in Ireland.

Relationships with Government Officials

Chinese society is socially stratified and class conscious. The social stratification is exercised through the bureaucratic system in China. Bureaucracy, as it is commonly accepted, 'hates change, is terrified by speed, and hates simplicity.'[15] Thus, to Irish business dealings, bureaucracy was found to be one problem that has caused inefficiency or even failure in Irish business dealings with China:

> With operating in China there are certain frustrations and difficulties and bureaucratic issues that you have to contend with. (H4)

> What I did find from my own experience, just getting away from the customer relationship, even dealing with the local bureaus and the different government agencies in China, a lot of people are aware it's a very bureaucratic process and it can be painful to try and get things done. For example, we tried to set up a trading company in China which, after a year-long registration process; a lot of that was down to inefficiency and bureaucracy within government departments and trying to get things processed and so forth. (H4)

Apart from bureaucracy, local governments' manipulation of central government policies also contributes to the complication and difficulty of doing business in China.

> Maybe government policies are not set in stone, that you can't demand things to be done or expect things to happen, because that's not the way things happen in China. You just have to go with the flow in a lot of cases. (H3)

Therefore, experienced Irish businesspeople have come to realise that building and maintaining a good relationship with government officials can be crucial for their business success in China.

> I think that maybe local contacts and building relationships with the local government are very important.... (H3)

> I know from anecdotal evidence that if you know somebody within the bureau or you can take them out to lunch or to dinner, the building of relationships can certainly ease your way. (H4)

Relationships with Business Partners

Most of the Irish businesspeople surveyed are aware that good business partners 'bridge the gap between the two cultures' and their chances of success would be significantly limited if they could not develop good relationships with Chinese business partners.

> I would say I'm only 6 per cent expert on the Chinese. They're that deep and it's that complex. You will never know them, so don't try to push it too far, and, you know, find somebody who can fill in the other 94 per cent. (CL15)

> Have an agent who could represent our interests honestly, industriously and efficiently. That was absolutely key to the success of the whole exercise. Without access to an agent who would actually do the travelling around the country, visit the factories, identify problems and advise us of those problems so that we could together ensure that they were solved, without that agent working on our behalf, I'm sure we would have had many more problems. By virtue of having that good agent, it actually increased our credibility with the manufacturers. (H5)

Irish businesspeople realise that it takes time to find a good agent in China and establish a good relationship with Chinese business partners. A businessman interviewee explained how he finally found a good partner after he had been doing business in China for six years:

> The usual interpreter was sick and they got this guy [for me]. He fully understood – he had perfect English – but more importantly, he was a budding businessman. So, he wasn't just interpreting, he was now interpreting but also emphasising what needed to be emphasised and then when he would be translating what the Chinese were saying, he would then be interpreting – 'they're saying this but I think they mean…' – and also, he became a very good way for me to be able to incentivise the other party without being the foreign devil, being directly involved …. And because he and I got on so well, we then became partners. (CL15)

Intercultural Marriages – The Role of Spouses and Partners

Intercultural marriage or partnership between an Irish businessman and a Chinese woman does not appear to be unusual in the world of Irish business in China. Although the total number remains unknown, more than one-quarter of the male interviewees turned out to have either a Chinese wife or a Chinese partner.

Such close personal relationships contribute to the development of a deep understanding of Chinese culture and society. When asked about the intercultural benefits of having a Chinese wife or partner, most interviewees' responses could be paraphrased as 'a deeper understanding of the Chinese mentality'. One interviewee claimed that such understanding has helped him deal with many complicated and difficult situations and achieve good success in his live seafood export/import business. Starting the business in China had been difficult; he felt frustrated and even considered giving it up. However, through his relationship with his wife he went through what he called his 'learning process' and came to realise:

> It [business success] is not going to happen overnight. I give a seminar to businessmen on how to give a business card. That's surface stuff. You've got to go right down deep, you know, right into the core of Chinese society and the culture and that takes a long time, a long time. (LV12)

His deeper understanding of Chinese culture and society changed his approach, leading him to recognise, 'You have to change for China – China doesn't change for you.' This helped him build up good relationships with his Chinese customers and achieve great success in the competitive fresh seafood market in China.

Relationships with Chinese People Living in Ireland

Irish companies and organisations recognise clear benefits from utilising the knowledge and skills of Chinese people who are resident in Ireland. In the higher education sector, for example:

> Having a Chinese expert, either on your staff or else as a consultant, can be very beneficial because, especially if you get somebody who has a background in the [Communist] Party or who has experience with government and so on, who understands a little bit more about [how] the system works, who speaks the language, that's very important, and who has connections. (H3)

Local Chinese people can be the first point of contact with China for Irish businesses. They can bring the Irish side into their circle of *guanxi*. As an entrepreneur interviewee put it:

> He or she [a member of Chinese community in Ireland] might know somebody who knows somebody who can help you. (V2)

Cultural Knowledge

Among the factors which respondents believe have contributed or will contribute to their business success in China, 'cultural knowledge' was ranked second, with 88 businesspeople out of 117 (76.5 per cent) responding to this item positively (see Chart 4).

Cultural knowledge is a broad category, including both general cultural knowledge and cultural knowledge of a particular area. Interviewees reported how their cultural knowledge in both of these senses helped them achieve business success in China.

General Cultural Knowledge

General knowledge of Chinese culture was found to be useful in building personal relationships with Chinese businesspeople, particularly with regard to those aspects of culture in which Irish and Chinese people share some common experience. The shared experience of foreign invasion and colonialism, together with a sensitivity and awareness of history, can help create a sense of closeness and trust. For example, an Irish businessman related how he had used his knowledge of Chinese and Irish history to secure a big contract with a Chinese company:

> In 1988, I was sitting in a hotel in Beijing and I was told by a Chinese guy I know, 'Ah, you just missed a big deal' and he named the company who were buying a freezer factory and he said, 'You just missed it. They've given the contract to someone else.' So, I got on a plane, went down to meet the company …. I explained to them the similarities between Ireland and China – that, you know, a thousand years ago, when the Europeans were all living like peasants, the Irish were the most educated. We were writing books and all this kind of stuff. We were the bastion of Christianity and we re-educated Europe. A thousand years ago, China was plotting the stars and doing all this wonderful art and all this kind

of thing and we were both developing nicely. And then we both, with the advent – I use the analogy of the advent of sailing ships, or powerful neighbours – came and began to damage us and because we weren't a warlike people, they were able to dominate us. In our case, it was the British, in your case, it was the Japanese. Similarly, at the beginning of the century, we both stood up and said, 'We want freedom…'. So, in 1921, we got our independence and in 1949, Lao Mao created the Revolution and here we are now. But what amazes me is that while we must never forget what happened, we find it difficult to forgive the English but you have clearly forgiven the Japanese – especially for what they did in this city of Nanjing. All the heads went down. I had the contract the next day. They cancelled the contract with Sanyo because I understood [their culture and feeling]. (CL15)

This is an amazing story in which his awareness of sharing similar historical experiences was able to create a sense of closeness with the Chinese businesspeople which, within 24 hours, transformed this Irish businessman from a complete stranger to an understanding and trustworthy business partner.

Knowledge of Business Culture

Having an understanding of Chinese business culture is recognised by Irish businesspeople as essential for doing business in and with China. A successful Irish business couple, for example, told us how they picked up a Chinese way – circuitous and indirect – to solve a problem without confrontation or loss of face:

I have another guy who makes cartons for me – he makes the cardboard boxes – and they're great. They're a really good factory – their work is great – but this particular guy is a difficult guy to deal with and … drives her [the Irish manager] crazy because he's not efficient …. One day, she got into a confrontation with him and I said to her, 'But this is the factory I'm going to buy my boxes from because they have the best ones and they have the best price and their service is very good … but the sales guy is difficult, for sure. [It] must [be] better for you to keep your relationship good with this guy and I'll talk to his boss the next time I'm there and try and – without actually complaining about this guy – try and see … his English is not so good and maybe I can say, do you have anyone else who has good English because often I need to have a direct correspondence, or whatever … and maybe that will be a way around the problem.' (CL13)

Another businessman said that he always got a contract signed smoothly by leaving his Chinese interpreter to chat with the Chinese company people after the formal negotiation finishes, just in case there might be a special request which the Chinese side would feel too embarrassed to ask for directly.

It might just be they would like a trip abroad but they don't want to say it to me because they would lose face. It could be a car. The companies we dealt with couldn't buy a car because they needed special permission to buy a car and they mightn't have had good enough reason to get that permission but if we gave them a car, we just added it onto the price of the deal – it didn't matter. It was that understanding. (CL15)

The knowledge of Chinese business culture has helped Irish business-people overcome the barrier caused by cultural distance and difference by adapting to Chinese ways of conducting business.

Understanding Institutional Aspects of the Chinese Market (Government Policies, Regulations, the Legal System and Business Law)

'Understanding of the Chinese market' was ranked third among the factors Irish businesspeople thought have contributed or will contribute to their success in their business dealings with China, with 78 respondents out of 115 (67.8 per cent) responding positively to this item (see Chart 4).

An important aspect of the Chinese market, according to what was discovered in our survey, concerns Chinese government policies, regulations, the legal system and business law. Irish businesspeople realise that China's rapidly expanding economy and fast-changing market are accompanied by many new government policies:

China's moving into high-end, high value-added products. Semi-conductors are an example. The Chinese enterprise income tax law was amended last year, respective from 1 January 2008, to give preferential tax treatment for those investing in research and development and those that meet certain environmentally friendly conditions. So, they are the two areas that China is focusing on: R&D [research and development] and environment-friendly industries. So, there's also preferential tax treatment for high-tech enterprises. You can qualify as a high-tech enterprise and pay a much lower – I think it's a 15 per cent – rate of tax. (LV9)

China is a highly regulated society, so every facet of business in China has applicable regulations – or most areas of business, in any event. There are always new regulations being brought out, existing regulations being revised or amended. This happens almost on a daily basis. (LV9)

Consequently, up-to-date information on these policies is indispensable for Irish companies and organisations to find new business opportunities and adjust their business strategies accordingly for the Chinese market.

Moreover, Irish businesspeople surveyed have recognised that one of the dynamics of Chinese business is that, in some cases, there are no fixed rules and regulations. They see this as both an advantage and a disadvantage in their business dealings with China. Once they get used to the Chinese flexibility they can find an easier and quicker way to solve problems. This is described as 'a very Chinese solution to a very Chinese problem'. However, for the Irish businesspeople who are new and immature in the Chinese market such flexibilities may frustrate them. They complain that the Chinese way is too flexible and see this as a barrier to doing business in or with China. Nevertheless, most Irish businesspeople surveyed agree that they are more flexible compared with Americans and some other Europeans; so it would not be too difficult for them to adapt to the Chinese practice of flexibility. This is further discussed in later sections.

Communication Skills

Among the factors Irish businesspeople identified as having contributed or would contribute to their success in their business dealings with China, 'communication skills' was ranked fourth, with 77 respondents out of 115 (67 per cent) responding positively to this item (see Chart 4).

Communication skills are those that enable a person to convey information so that it is received and understood. In the context of the business culture that we are emphasising, communication skills are related to cultural awareness and understanding. In the Chinese business environment, as many Irish businesspeople surveyed suggested, business success heavily relies on personal relationships. This makes an understanding of Chinese cultural concepts in relation to person-to-person communication one of the keys to achieving business success. For example, Chinese people dislike confrontation, they wish to protect 'face' (how they are viewed within the community), they respect authority, and they distrust strangers; understanding of these can help improve communication skills.

> [When having a negative opinion], you have to say 'that's a very interesting proposal, something that we haven't considered before, we need to consult with the powers that be back in Ireland (or wherever) and we'll get back to you…' and then you can discuss other points around that main point, which might be a possible compromise, but you can't say 'no' – you can't out-and-out say 'no, that is totally unacceptable' …. There's all these differences that need to be borne in mind. (LV9)

Even in cases where Chinese partners or employees do something wrong and an Irish boss or manager has justification to react with criticism, an indirect or diplomatic way to communicate with the person concerned is still required.

> I find that when I write an email now, having experienced this [that Chinese people are circuitous and dislike confrontation] for a few years, I write an email – if I'm criticising – I write it very differently than I would have written it five years ago; very differently. It's very diplomatic. Absolutely … you encourage them to find solutions, rather than just criticise, without the other elements in it. In fact, actually, it's only now that I'm talking about it, I realise that I write emails very diplomatically and we've instructed the staff how to write emails, having seen that they sometimes do it wrong as well, you know. (CL13)

It is also realised that Chinese employees often feel reluctant to present their opinion frankly in a meeting due to the fear of losing face so special communication skills have to be used.

They very often in meetings don't confide in you; they tend to be very reserved and hide their feelings and they are not open to discuss things that might be bothering them and so on. So prior to having a meeting I like to be able to spend time with them one-on-one, talk about things that I see, and when I do spend time one-on-one with them, they are more open and then it is my job to kind of in effect help them save face and not point out 'Joe said this', 'Susan was not doing this correctly' or whatever. Instead of saying that, I will say, 'I've seen that this is an issue' or 'This is an area where we could do something better' or whatever so I, in turn, communicate the kinds of things that I want to see enhanced or changed or whatever and I still solicit the input from everybody on an individual basis and then when I come to the meeting I need to be prepared to be able to talk about those things and do it in a way that I'm not causing anybody to lose face and be able to help get changes too from the top down. (F1)

In order to promote a less confrontational atmosphere, some business-men will even change their seating positions in meetings with a Chinese customer and make themselves look more like a neutral broker.

And even if I was on my own, I would never sit opposite any-body. I'll always try to sit here, you know … because in a way, you're manipulating the stage, so that it appears to be less con frontational. (CL15)

Access to Information Sources

Access to information sources was thought to be an important issue by the Irish businesspeople surveyed. Among the factors which the Irish businesspeople think have contributed or will contribute to their business success in China, more than half of respondents (59 out of 115, 51.3 per cent) responded positively regarding 'access to information sources' (see Chart 4).

For most Irish companies and organisations, the Chinese market is new, fast-changing and different from the European and American mar-kets which they may be used to dealing with. Geographical and cultural differences, the language barrier and lack of expertise can all contribute to the blockage of information channels and make the Chinese market appear strange and inaccessible. Some Irish companies and organisations have found that up-to-date information is inaccessible in Ireland.

> There's no information available in Ireland for Irish people doing business in China. There just isn't. The information isn't there. And they can't look up Chinese websites. Most of their computers aren't even able to read Chinese characters. Even if they were able to, if their software was able to enable Chinese characters, they wouldn't be able to read it anyway. You know what? It's almost like it's too much of an effort … too complicated. (LV9)

Thus, the Irish businesspeople surveyed claimed that access to information sources is the key to their business success. The remedy some interviewees found and recommended to solve this problem is to set up a representative office in China. Such offices were described as 'the eyes and ears of their business in China'. Slightly more than half of the Irish companies and organisations surveyed, 50.4 per cent, have a physical business presence in China (49.6 per cent don't); this was believed to be beneficial to their business dealings with China. Among the respondents who claimed that information scarcity was a problem preventing them from achieving greater success in doing business in or with China, more than half of these had no physical presence in China (see Chart 6).

Furthermore, when those surveyed were asked to identify the factors which have contributed or will contribute to their business success in China, positive responses to 'understanding market', 'good personal relationships' and 'communication skills' of 73.7 per cent, 93 per cent and 68.4 per cent respectively are shown among those who have representative offices in China, while the percentage of positive responses among those without offices in China are lower, at 60.7 per cent, 75 per cent and 66.1 per cent respectively (see Chart 5). The figures indicate that having a physical presence in China may provide an Irish company or organisation with one of the best channels to receive up-to-date information that can help them to better understand the Chinese market.

Language Ability

Many Chinese people are fluent in the English language. Consequently there is the expectation that foreign businesspeople who intend to build long-term business relationships in China should make a reasonable effort to learn the Chinese language. The case can be made that

Irish people are developing a better attitude to learning languages than in the past.

Among the factors which Irish businesspeople thought have contributed or will contribute to their business success in China, 47 out of 115 respondents (40.9 per cent) indicated that 'language ability' was important (see Chart 4).

Native Language Competency Not Major Concern

The above relatively low percentage indicates that language ability in Chinese is not considered by the majority of Irish companies and organisations as essential to achieve business success in China. Through our interview survey, three main reasons have been identified for this:

1. English is used as a common working language in Chinese business sectors
2. Businesspeople often take advantage of speaking English in business dealings
3. Many businesspeople think it is more important to understand Chinese culture and history than learning the Chinese language

English as a Common Working Language

English is the most popular foreign language in China, and usually Chinese business partners can either speak relatively good English themselves or find an interpreter to assist. Therefore, the language barrier is less of a major consideration for many Irish companies and organisations.

> For business, the language barrier is not a major consideration because the Chinese will be familiar with English and it is the Chinese that are usually selling the products or services – products, anyway – and so they will have a vested interest in being able to speak English. (LV9)

For some Irish businesspeople, translation services are even provided after work:

> I think even after one or two years most of them [Irish business-people] had very basic Chinese; it was never a priority, it was never a necessity, because they had the support structure around them to help them do their shopping, and taxis everywhere .... (H3)

Therefore, for many Irish companies and organisations, language would not be thought of as a problem preventing them from getting business done in China:

> [Language] is not particularly a problem because they will always find somebody that can help them out. They'll always be able to find somebody to assist them in getting business done; that's never a problem, I don't think. (LV9)

Taking Advantage of Speaking English in Business Dealings

Some Irish businesspeople have developed good language skills in Chinese over time but they would not use it in business situations. They use the speaking of English to their advantage in their business dealings. One interviewee, who can speak fluent Chinese, explained why he has never used it on business occasions:

> Number one: a white guy speaking Chinese … just means (I am a) poor student; but if you speak English, it's a rich businessman …. Number two: if I keep a meeting in English, I control the environment … like now. I'm much more comfortable speaking to you guys in English because it's my native tongue, so I can take the lead …. [Number three]: it gives me time to respond with the proper answer – a suitable answer. It's not cheating. Most of our clients in business, most of my clients, know that I speak Chinese. They do know, but they do respect that I want to speak English. (LV12)

Focusing on Culture and History

Some Irish businesspeople felt learning the Chinese language is not as important as understanding Chinese culture and history. Chinese is difficult and time-consuming to learn, so their limited time could be better spent focusing on culture and history instead. For example, the businessman who convinced a Chinese company to cancel a big contract with the Japanese and give it to him instead (see above) commented:

> Now, they [the Chinese party] didn't even know I existed at that time but within 24 hours, they cancelled the contract with the Japanese and they gave it to us …. I took the view early on that, rather than trying to learn the Chinese language, I would focus

on the culture and the history because the language is so difficult …
it's so difficult. It's very all-consuming. (CL15)

Competence of the Interpreter

Since English is the commonly used working language, 51 respondents
out of 115 (44.3 per cent) thought a good interpreter had made or
would make a contribution to business success in China (see Chart 4).

Successful Irish companies and organisations were found to be always
cautious about the quality of interpreters, and to believe that it was
important to make sure that interpreters translate accurately and
impartially:

> There were some of them who were very good at that. Not
> everybody. There were some of the interpreters who not only
> told you what the other person said, but told you what the other
> person was feeling when they said it, and that was very, very
> beneficial to understand that the person was concerned or the
> person was angry, or that kind of thing, to be able to understand
> where they were coming from. (F1)

Some companies and organisations even avoid using an interpreter
provided by the other side they are dealing with:

> I would always advocate [Irish businesspeople] using their own
> interpreter, rather than [that of] the person you're trying to deal
> with because, you know, at least you can say what you want to say
> and not what he wants hear …. Quite often, the interpreter from
> his side can interpret what he wants to hear. (LV11)

Knowing Chinese Is Beneficial for Building Up Personal Relations

Chinese people do not generally expect the foreigner to be able to
communicate in Chinese, but may be very pleasantly surprised if the
foreigner shows an interest in the Chinese language and culture, and has
made an effort to learn how to exchange greetings in Chinese. This can
not only be of practical usefulness, but also have a very positive effect
on personal relations:

> I find that if you manifest the slightest interest in Chinese culture
> to a Chinese person, especially if you speak a bit of Chinese – this

35

was true even when I first arrived in China and my Chinese was absolutely terrible, you know – the slightest bit of genuine interest and effort is welcomed. They don't fully expect you will have that (CL17).

Although English is a commonly used working language, a lack of language ability in speaking Chinese is viewed by some Irish businesspeople as having a negative impact on the personal relationship between the parties:

> It's not that you don't trust them on a personal level, it's that you don't trust that they fully understand what you're going to do or how the transaction is going to work and then also … because in China, business is driven by the personal relationship between the two parties, it means that if you don't speak the language, then that has a negative impact on the personal relationship between the parties. (LV9)

Thus, they tried to speak to local people in Chinese outside work and it was found to be beneficial for making connections:

> When we are having a business dinner or a networking thing, I would try to talk in Chinese just to make that connection, just to make that effort. That is always important ….You can always talk about drink as well. It is always a staple topic of conversation. (F2)

In certain work fields, knowledge of Chinese is of great practical value. One Irish lawyer described how his Chinese language ability enabled him to perform a very useful professional function and improve the performance of the company:

> I was kind of there as a guest and extremely well treated, as you'd expect in Chinese culture as a guest, but also quite a useful guest. Thankfully I have a decent amount of Chinese so I could work slowly but I could work directly with Chinese documents – with a lot of help from the dictionary – and I can communicate with my Chinese colleagues through – well, let's call it a mix of English and Chinese – but I try to get the Chinese to dominate. The firm were taking on a lot of trainees, sorry interns, who would come

in for a few weeks and there would be a relationship-building exercise. If you don't have any Chinese they'd be sitting at the desk finding things to do, pushing paper around the desk most of the time. So it was a very good experience for everyone involved, it built up relationships, for the guest to have a bit of Chinese experience. I think it was precisely because I had some Chinese and I was able to translate documents – not into Chinese but from Chinese – I could read a memo in Chinese and say if it made sense and so on. And obviously I could help with their English. It was the largest law firm in China and a lot of their clients would be international corporations investing in China and they would expect their memos in English. It was Chinese law advice but they would expect their memos to be written in English, so I'm sure you're aware there is a very big language barrier there. So my function – the way I made myself useful at first – was very much by bridging that language barrier. I would help them say what they meant to say by chatting with the people who wrote them or looking at the original. (CL17)

Thus, although language skill may not be viewed as an essential factor for many Irish businesspeople to achieve success in China, it does play an important role in their business dealings and relationship building. In some business contexts, such as a law firm, Chinese language skills can be very valuable.

Irish Social Networks in China

Several interviewees mentioned attending Irish social and cultural events, as well as taking part in various sporting clubs and occasions in China. For the purposes of this report, the presence of interconnected communities of Irish businesspeople in Chinese cities is of interest as these social links not only enable individuals to get to know each other, but also come into contact with each other's networks and share business information. One young middle manager noted that the Irish networks in China were at an earlier stage of development compared to those in other parts of Asia:

I think there is a greater potential there for Irish companies to help each other out in this market, because when you do any business here, you do rely on lots of other businesses, whether is it just some connector there that facilitates relying on another Irish company, or whether another Irish company can put you into contact with other Chinese companies that can help you out, there is an opportunity there to facilitate. (F2)

With figures for Irish citizens in China who have registered at the Embassy of Ireland in Beijing numbering in the hundreds rather than the thousands,[16] it may be estimated that a few thousand Irish people at most are present in the country, to include those who have not chosen to register themselves and other 'diaspora' Irish who hold passports of other countries while cherishing their identity and links to home.

However, alongside the growing interest in Ireland about China, it seems there is correspondingly some measure of increasing recognition and curiosity among Chinese people regarding Irish culture. Ireland's unique status as a very small yet English-speaking Western country that 'no one sees … as a threat' because 'it doesn't have an agenda' may have begun to carve out a distinct identity for Ireland in China.[17] Officially sanctioned and approved Saint Patrick's Day parades in Shanghai (from 2007) and Beijing (from 2008), for example, although relatively small in comparison to much bigger events elsewhere in the world, are unusual in the Chinese context, where 'foreign' parades are far from the norm. 'Irishness' in this form is able to be celebrated openly and its warm invitation to join in is generally easily welcomed and accepted. Irish-themed pubs, many with real Irish connections and some with actual Irish management, are now found throughout China (in large urban settings). Such establishments, in addition to attracting locals and people from all over the world, also provide Irish people with places to meet and socialise with each other and their friends, colleagues and associates. Irish Network China (www.irish networkchina.com) organises informal monthly gatherings of the Irish community and friends in Beijing Irish pubs, for example (as well as numerous other charity events and social activities – their website provides links to other Irish bodies active in China, including Enterprise Ireland, the Ireland China Association, Irish Abroad and the Irish Business Forum Shanghai).

Another notable twenty-first century development is the Asian County Board GAA. A vibrant and growing Gaelic sports-based social network has been evolving in China with links to this continent-wide 'county' organisation. In an Irish pub in Beijing, however, one interviewee explained why he had been reluctant at first to play Gaelic sports in China:

> I played Gaelic here two summers, but I was never good enough to take it really seriously! They are positive; it is just, I suppose, a lot of people come here to get away from that, initially anyway they come to have a different kind of life to what they have at home, so they are not going to come straight to the Irish bar and they are not going to do Gaelic. It wasn't until after a year and a half, with some prodding from certain people who were interested in doing it, that I joined in. (F2)

The implication is that when Irish people first arrive in China, they may hold the understandable belief that joining a GAA club is not an obvious way to make contact with Chinese people and culture. Later, they may find that such organisations are able to provide a forum in which Irish and Chinese people can meet and get to know each other better.

These clubs are open, sociable organisations in China, with Irish, Chinese and many other nationalities represented in their membership. Another young middle-level manager described his local club as full of what he identified as the 'Irish spirit' of friendliness and welcome, and commented that not only was the Irish business community in his city linked through the GAA club, but that some of their Chinese friends and business contacts also enjoyed participating.[18] The focus is not necessarily always on serious sporting competition, while at the same time matches and social events are organised both within China and also across the even more vast expanse of Asia, with teams from as far apart as the Arabian peninsula states, Thailand, Malaysia, Singapore, Vietnam, Taiwan, Indonesia and Japan competing with each other. In China, these Gaelic sports clubs and other Irish-based networks are forming intercultural communities, bringing Irish people in contact with each other and each other's friends and associates of whatever nationality. The list of clubs includes Shanghai Saints and Sirens, Dalian GAA, Shenzhen Celts, Beijing GAA, Hong Kong GAA and Guangzhou Celts, who describe themselves as 'the only Gaelic team in the world with just one Irish player and he never turns up anyway'. Such light-hearted humour is typical of Asian 'County' Board clubs and how they present themselves. Further information on the Asian County Board GAA with useful links to the Chinese clubs can be found at www.asiancountyboard.com.

SIMILARITIES AND DIFFERENCES BETWEEN IRISH AND CHINESE BUSINESS CULTURES

The questionnaire asked two particular questions concerning perceptions of similarities and differences between Irish and Chinese culture. The questions were designed based on initial research work in which some similarities were identified, and consequently the question arose as to whether an awareness of these similarities might offer Irish businesspeople some advantage in their business dealings with China.

The first question asked was, 'Do you think Chinese culture shares more similarities with Irish culture than it does with other European cultures or with American culture?' To this question, 43.3 per cent of respondents responded positively, with 8.8 per cent saying they 'strongly agree' and 34.5 per cent 'agree', while 25.7 per cent responded to it negatively, with 19.5 per cent registering 'disagree' and 6.2 per cent 'strongly disagree'. The remainder, 31 per cent, chose 'do not know' (see Chart 7). The very wide spread of opinion begged the question, why was there such variation in response to this question?

The relatively large percentage of 'do not know' answers, together with the fact that many interviewees' initial response to this question was 'I am not too sure' or 'I really don't know', may show that a sizeable proportion of Irish businesspeople either had not given much thought to this comparison before or were not sure how to answer because of conflicting indications. The question itself is complex because to be in a position to give an informed answer the respondent needed to be confident of his/her comparisons and understanding not only of Chinese culture, but also of European and American cultures. However, to the second question, which asked questionnaire participants to rank what they consider to be the degree of similarity between Irish and Chinese cultures, the percentage of positive responses was much higher. A similar phenomenon was observed in how interviewees responded when discussing cultural issues. As conversations on culture proceeded, more similarities were identified and recognised by the respondents.

This indicates that for some Irish businesspeople, their perception of similarities and differences between Irish and Chinese culture remains somewhat hidden within their consciousness. In their experience of business dealings with China, many had learned to adjust their approaches and even to adopt aspects of Chinese cultural behaviour into their business practice. But it seemed that many had not consciously connected their Irish cultural background to their social adaptability or considered whether their own cultural attributes might have helped them accept Chinese culture more easily than businesspeople from other European countries or from America; nor, apparently, were most respondents aware that by taking advantage of the similarities between Irish and Chinese culture they might become more competitive, and in a much better position to achieve greater success in the Chinese market.

Very Similar

Of the nine cultural aspects listed in our questionnaire, four were ranked as 'very similar' with relatively high percentages: 'do business through personal connections' (56.8 per cent, 63 out of 111), 'use long-term relationships to establish mutual trust' (48.2 per cent, 53 out of 110), 'highly values friendship' (46.8 per cent, 52 out of 111) and 'focus on family values' (45.9 per cent, 50 out of 109) (see Chart 8).

Socio-Historical Background

These four cultural aspects (personal connections, long-term relationships, friendship and family values) are all related to the primacy of human relations, which is a core concept in traditional Chinese thought and Confucianism. Thus, it is interesting to see the above questions in relation to this concept being given an overwhelming positive response by a group of businesspeople whose country is geographically and culturally distant from China. The businesspeople surveyed who claimed that the Irish were different from other Europeans and from Americans may have had a sense of what had been experienced in the past as well as of their sociocultural environment. The long period of living as an agricultural society, the sufferings under English colonial rule, the trad-ition of emigration and Ireland's geographical isolation from the European continent have all contributed to the unique Irish character. Some of this contributes to the Irish culture sharing some similarities with other cultures outside the sociocultural context of Europe and America. As interviewees suggested:

> Rural societies are probably much closer to one another than the rural societies and the urban societies in the same country. So I think if you went back 50 years to rural Ireland you'd find a lot of the Irish would be much closer to the way China is now, and

in some ways closer than rural China is to Shanghai or Beijing, because so much of life revolves around agriculture … (VR1)

Because of our nature and personal character, we have a lot more in common with the Chinese when we would be sitting across the table from them [than] perhaps our French or our German or our Scandinavian, or even in many instances our British, counterparts; they tend to relate better to Irish businesspeople than they do [to] people from those countries. I should also include North America, who don't have the same degree of spontaneity and personality that we would have. The Chinese connect with us very quickly I have found. (LV9)

Similarities in Cultural Position of Human Relations

In the past, in both Irish and Chinese society, social organisation and social relations were primarily established and developed on the basis of patriarchal families; the influence of such traditions should never be underestimated. In Ireland, for example, up until 2005 as many as 90 per cent of Irish firms were still being identified as family firms.[19] Some of our interviewees confirmed this, that relatives and relations of friends commonly have senior management positions in Chinese companies:

So in large companies, my experience when I was first here is that the top people in the organisation very often are brothers, cousins, friends who grew up in the same, you know, hometown, in the same neighbourhood, that kind of thing, and that trickles down. It is true in the police department; it is true in every organisation I've seen here. (F1)

A similar social concept and practice was acknowledged by the Irish businesspeople surveyed. They see themselves as sharing more in common with Chinese people than with others in terms of the way they view family, friendship and personal connections:

There's a lot of emphasis in Ireland on family. Probably the most important part of anybody's life in Ireland. It's always been like that in Ireland. We haven't suffered the social collapse that Britain has suffered. (LV9)

I think Ireland has a lot more in common with China than people think and I think a lot of that has to do with the family structure, because people are very family focused in China and I think in Ireland, they still are. It's changing but it's still … like in mainland Europe, where the family is largely still there but it's much different. People are much more individually focused, rather than family focused, whereas in Ireland, there's still a family consciousness. That's one thing that's a definite similarity. People are very loyal to their parents; that's very important …. (VL10)

The Chinese go back to the cultural aspect of family, you know, and if you get to know a Chinese [person] very well and you get on with them and … you do business, they lead you to their family and introduce you to their home … that is a very good achievement, you know. (CL16)

Some Irish businesspeople may not see much similarity between Irish culture and Chinese culture, but they do recognise that family is equally important in both cultures:

Other than family values, that the family is quite important to both, I wouldn't say there is a huge amount of cultural similarities. (H3)

The cultural similarities create a sense of closeness and trust between Irish and Chinese, which has helped Irish businesspeople achieve greater success in their business dealings with China.

We'd be seen as being closer to the Chinese than would other foreigners. Psychologically, we'd be closer. They don't need to do business with us but they choose to do business with us, whereas they need to do business with the other people. (CL15)

Some Irish businesspeople see being family orientated as one means of finding a common ground of humanity and appealing to what is held to be good and moral:

You should be able to take advantage of the good that is out there and the good that is here in China, and if you present yourself as being that kind of person, as being family oriented and recognising the value that they place on that as well, that will help you to inter-act with them and, you know, anyone who comes here who is prejudiced against others, regardless of where they are from and so on, that will be perceived to make you be not a good person. (F1)

Little Similarity

Of nine cultural aspects listed in our questionnaire, three were ranked as 'very similar' by very small minorities of respondents and as having 'little similarity' by between a third and just over a half:

- 'Respects/obeys authority', with 3.7 per cent of respondents ranking it as 'very similar' but 36.1 per cent as having 'little similarity'
- 'Importance of saving face/avoiding losing face', with 5.5 per cent of respondents ranking it as 'very similar' but 53.6 per cent as having 'little similarity'
- 'Flexible in following regulations', with 12 per cent of respondents ranking it as 'very similar' but 34.3 per cent as having 'little similarity' (see Chart 8).

Respects/Obeys Authority

It can be seen that concerning certain cultural features, Irish businesspeople consider themselves to be very different from Chinese. For example, Irish businesspeople have noticed that there is rarely an open challenge to formal authority in China and the important decisions made at the top of the ladder in the highly structured society are not open for debate.

> There would be, generally speaking, a respect for authority in Ireland but nowhere close to the same extent as there would be in China. From my experiences and from anecdotal stories I have been told from others, there is a much higher respect for authority in China, and even if I was talking to one of my subordinates and genuinely ask their opinion on something, or asking if they agree or not, they would actually be afraid to tell me that they didn't agree with me; not afraid, but they would feel like they were challenging me, whereas with my boss in Ireland I wouldn't hesitate if I felt that something wasn't right in my opinion, I wouldn't hesitate in saying it. To me, it's not disrespectful; it's just voicing an opinion. (H4)

> What I learned over time, working with these people, was that if you want to effect a change in an organisation, you have to do it from the top down ….When we have meetings they expect you to drive the process. They very often in meetings don't confide in you, they tend to be very reserved and hide their feelings and they are not open to discuss things that might be bothering them and so on …. (F1)

Sometimes, this mentality can cause serious misunderstandings between an Irish boss and a Chinese subordinate and create problems which could otherwise have been avoided:

> I think there is a higher degree of respect for managers from subordinates, I think subordinates would tend, from my experience, not to speak their mind, even if they have …. I mean I have had the situation where I took on one of my co-workers and for a period of a number of months she was busy and she was stressed, and I suppose everyone was because it was a busy time for the company, and then at one point she said that she was thinking of quitting, that she felt everything was a bit overwhelming and I said 'If you have felt like this, why didn't you come and talk to me two months previously?' That would typically be the case in Ireland. (H4)

The answer the Chinese employee gave to the Irish boss reflects a completely different way of thinking:

> When I asked her why she didn't speak to me two months ago, she said 'I didn't want to bother you, you were busy. I didn't want to create problems for you.' I said to her, 'It's more of a problem if you decide to leave tomorrow.' (H4)

Such experience makes Irish businesspeople aware that the Chinese system is based on strict hierarchies and an almighty bureaucracy which are strikingly different from that in Irish society. The deeply-rooted tradition can be traced back to Confucius, who initiated the notion of social classification to maintain a political order of feudalism which was constantly reinforced by the rulers of almost all regimes in China over a period of more than two thousand years.

Moreover, the concept of hierarchy and respecting and obeying authority is intimately related to another concept – face. As a huge issue in China, face can sometimes appear to conflict with Western ideas of equality and openness.

The Importance of Saving Face/Avoiding Losing Face

The most important rule of social interaction in China is always to give face, to save face, and never to lose face. Saving face is not such a strange concept in Irish society, where fear of an embarrassing, disgraceful or compromising situation also exists. However, Irish businesspeople find the concept of face is valued much more highly in China than it is in Ireland. One business couple interviewed, for example, viewed cultural similarities between Irish and Chinese people very positively, but the face issue was seen as the biggest single difference:

> I think most things are quite similar … but the biggest single diff-erence, I think, has to do with the face issue. If I had to pick one thing – the face issue. I think that's the biggest single difference. If I had to pick one thing, that's the one I'd pick. (LV13)

This view is shared by many Irish businesspeople with experience of respecting face in China.

> It's just so important in the Chinese context, they are very proud people, they don't like to be shown up; again the same could be said of anyone. Nobody likes to be, not even shown up, but there are certain practices in China: you don't contradict somebody, you don't say somebody is wrong in front of a crowd of people, there are just rules you have to observe in China whereas that wouldn't be the case in Ireland. (H4)

Therefore Irish businesspeople find that open criticism and challenging decisions made by authority are among the most obvious violations of Chinese norms. For Chinese people, giving face is one of the best ways to show respect and obedience to authorities and the worst situation is to cause people in a senior position to lose face. This is why Chinese people would not usually present their opinion frankly or directly in a meeting organised by a senior manager or during a negotiation with a foreign company. In such situations, presenting a negative opinion is regarded as a serious offence against the person in charge, or the person one is doing business with.

> Well, again because the infrastructure above them was typically this who-knows-who kind of an infrastructure, whatever proce-dures and processes existed in [an] organisation were established by these people who-know-who; and there is another facet of the infrastructure that exists here and it is throughout China, it is in personal dealings as well as in business dealings – is that saving face is a huge, huge factor in terms of how people deal with each

other, in terms of how business gets done, and like I say even though some of these younger middle-management people were very intelligent and very well educated, some had doctorate degrees and that kind of thing, they are not able to challenge what exists procedurally or process-wise in an organisation because the who-know-who people established those procedures and if something gets challenged going up the ladder, somebody could potentially lose face. (F1)

They also find that making a decision or solving a problem without requesting instructions from authority are considered by the Chinese as offensive and face-losing. Thus, the Chinese are always reluctant to make decisions or find a solution to problems on their own, even if they are experienced and capable of doing so. Chinese people are often found to withhold their feelings, opinions and views:

Certainly the types of questions that they were coming to me with were so fundamental, I had no doubt they were intelligent enough to figure it out for themselves. There was no question that they hadn't the ability or they hadn't the intelligence; it was almost a reluctance to want to make a decision, or to try and find a solution to something. (H4)

The Chinese don't like to be frank. By frank, I mean, many Chinese people would keep back their feelings about something, rather than expressing it openly. (LV15)

Therefore, Irish businesspeople must realise that they have to be extremely patient in the process of discussion and negotiation:

Direct is the way to deal with them, but they don't come directly in negotiations, they are very circuitous as to how they come to a final point in negotiations, and you have to expect that, and respect it, when you find that the whole negotiation process has come to nothing because nothing has actually been agreed when you thought it had. Don't allow yourself to be frustrated; be patient and be patient again, and then be even more patient. When the trip comes to an end and you haven't achieved what you needed to achieve, don't be frustrated; you should have gone in anticipation of that happening and knowing that a second trip will be required. Things don't happen overnight and I think a lot of Western companies get frustrated and they don't give the task the degree of tolerance and patience that it requires. It really requires endless, boundless patience. (H5)

Flexibility in Following Regulations

The other cultural issue which is viewed by Irish businesspeople as different from their own culture is being 'flexible in following regulations'. As discussed earlier, Irish people do recognise that there exists a certain flexibility in Irish society and compared with people from other European countries or the USA, the Irish see themselves as more flexible. However, they think flexibility is far greater in the Chinese sociocultural context. On the one hand, there is a large body of regulations and laws established in contemporary China; on the other hand, however, Chinese people do not strictly follow all the rules. Finding a solution outside regulations and laws is still a common practice in the context of Chinese business culture.

> Well, contracts are important, of course, but what's more important is the trust and the relationship between the parties. So, if the Chinese party, for example, is unable to meet a deadline when the excuse is good, they will explain to you what the problem is, assume that you understand and they don't expect you to start imposing penalties or fines, etcetera, even if the contract says that. They say that you should understand what has happened, that we'll try our best to complete the deal and complete the transaction. In other words, I think in Ireland, or in Europe, it's the contracts that determine everything in the parties. (LV9)

This is a typical Chinese way to solve a problem whereby despite violation of the formal contract, interpersonal trust plays a key role in maintaining good contractual relationships between two business parties. Thus Irish businesspeople may find that although most newly issued Chinese regulations and laws are similar in form to those in Western countries, their actual implementation and application can be affected by a different mentality.

> I would say in China there are a lot more regulations and if you follow the letter of the law in everything life would be very difficult. My boss always says that there is a Chinese solution to a

Chinese problem, that without doing anything illegal there are always ways. (H4)

In the application of laws, the traditional Chinese approach is still influential, in which disputes are expected to be settled by mediators rather than brought to a court; only when both parties are prepared to ruin their relationship do they go to a court and sue.

> And also the belief that any problem can be overcome, just by talking and trying to find a solution and resolving … that's why mediation is so important in China and that's why you have organisations like the China International Economic and Trade Commission and the Beijing Arbitration Commission, which also specialises in mediation services. In China, if you sue, that is completely the end of the relationship, whereas in Ireland if you sue, the lawsuit relates to a specific transaction and does not necessarily mean the end to the business relationship. But in China, to sue is really the last resort. (LV9)

These excerpts from experienced businesspeople suggest that under-standing the way Chinese people follow regulations and laws is even more important than understanding the regulations and laws them-selves. Most experienced Irish businesspeople find that strictly following rules in the sense of taking a legalistic approach to solving problems may lead to business failure in China, as it blocks the channel of negotiation at the person-to-person level, which is key to solving problems. Therefore, a large number of respondents see a big difference between the Irish and the Chinese in relation to their flexibility in following regulations.

Some Similarity

Surprisingly, all nine cultural aspects listed in our questionnaire were ranked as having 'some similarity' by between 40 per cent and 60 per cent of our respondents, including the above three issues (view on authority, saving face and flexibility), which are viewed by the majority of Irish businesspeople as sharing little similarity with Chinese people (see Chart 8).

This result raises an interesting question: how do Irish businesspeople go about looking at cultural similarities and differences?

Chinese–Irish Cultural Comparisons in the Context of Other Western Cultures

Many interviewees presented their views on the issue of cultural similarities and differences differently when other cultures in addition to those of Ireland and China were included in the question. When they compared Irish culture with Chinese culture directly they would see more differences than similarities, aware that the two cultures have developed in geographically, historically and politically different environments and involve many different sociocultural concepts. However, when they included a comparison of Irish culture with other European cultures or American culture, they recognised that they are different from other foreign cultures in contact with China and began to see more similarities than differences with Chinese culture.

For example, one businessman saw a lot of differences when he compared Irish and Chinese culture, highlighting such notions as face, hierarchy, importance of relationships and so on.

> In terms of doing business, I think politeness probably plays a much more, or the semblance of politeness, it is sort of this face and the euphemisms and so on, would play quite an important part which perhaps people don't realise ….Working in China, or with Asians in general, understanding the rules of politeness as they exist out here, understanding the notions of hierarchy, understanding the nature and the importance of relationships, and understanding the differences and the advantages and disadvantages of being direct or being indirect, and all of these other types of notions. (F3)

However, when looking at the issues and wondering whether Irish people, as distinct from any other nationality, have any particular cultural values or norms which work well with Chinese people, he talked in terms of a bridge from Ireland to China that jumps over America or the rest of Europe:

> I think that there do exist quite a few [similarities] actually! It is like there is a bridge from Ireland to China that either jumps over the United States or jumps over the rest of Europe, kind of a bypass as it were. I will mention the positive things. I think that both [the] Irish and [the] Chinese are very gregarious and very sociable people; again another one of these clichés that Irish people love socialising in bars. I suppose, in China, the restaurant

would be the forum of choice, and alcohol would play quite a preponderant role in these types of meetings and dinners. (F3)

Another businessman identified Irish culture as being more similar to Chinese culture when comparing it with America and the rest of Europe.

I'd say that it's similar, in the sense that people are open and friendly. Irish people are the most open and the most friendly and most hospitable people you could ever meet. Really. Irish people in general, are open, friendly and hospitable. They have a name around the world for being like that, you know. In China, you know, people are like that. They're very open, friendly and hospitable. Chinese people … if you had any sort of trouble, they'd always help you. I wouldn't say it's the same in Europe. So, Chinese people are more open, more friendly and more hospitable. (LV9)

The comparison suggests Irish businesspeople see certain distinctions in being Irish and are able to turn this to their advantage in doing business in or with China in a way which English or American businesspeople may not have the same opportunity to do:

We're not English, we're not American – we're Irish and there is an advantage there, doing business in some countries, and China is one of them. (CL16)

Irish perceptions of commonalities with Chinese culture were reflected in the questionnaire survey results. For example, although the Irish businesspeople interviewed realised that there are big differences between Irish and Chinese culture with regard to respecting and obeying authority, saving face and flexibility in following regulations, many still ranked these as having 'some similarity'. For these China-experienced people, Chinese culture may represent one extreme while American and some other European cultures may represent the other; Irish culture is perceived as standing somewhere in between. For example, as discussed earlier, Irish businesspeople think they are less flexible in following rules than the Chinese, but more flexible than Americans and other Europeans. By Irish standards, Chinese people are considered to be indeed more flexible in following regulations and laws:

'Flexibility in [following] regulations': my thought on that is that there are far more regulations in China but they wouldn't be as rigorously enforced as they would be in Ireland. I would say Ireland is less regulated but probably more forcefully regulated. (H4)

However, compared with other Europeans and Americans, Irish people would consider themselves different in the sense that it is easier for them to undergo certain cultural adaptations, for example by adopting flexibility in following regulations and laws:

> I mean advantage and disadvantage. I mean the Germans work in that way for reasons because they know it is the most efficient way of working, and in a way it is, and when you are trying to deal with Chinese companies that can be evasive and promise the world of one thing, and then the next meeting you have they say 'Oh, we never said anything like that'; when you have systems that a German operates on or a Dutch operates on, then it can be beneficial that way, but if you don't come halfway, then you are always asking for trouble in that way, and that is what the Irish are particularly good at. (F2)

Irish businesspeople admit that Chinese flexibility can be a drawback in the sense that it may sometimes cause lower efficiency and suspicion or distrust between the two business parties. However, they can also see advantages in flexibility which enables problems to be solved – sometimes in an easier or more efficient way. It may be because of the mixture of both positive and negative opinion on the issue that the majority of questionnaire participants ranked 'flexibility in following regulations' as having 'some similarity' with Irish business culture.

The Impact of Length of Time Doing Business in or with China

The length of time doing business in or with China may also contribute to Irish businesspeople's views about the similarity/difference issue. From the data shown in Table 2, it can be seen that the respondents who have been doing business in China for more than twelve months but less than three years tended to be more positive about similarities in certain cultural attributes, such as respecting and obeying authority, saving face and flexibility in following regulations. A higher percentage of these indicated 'some similarity' than those who have been doing business in China for more than three years. Having overcome initial culture shock and distance, it appears that these people began to notice more similarities between Chinese and Irish cultures. Those who were

Table 2: Cross Tabulation of Q20 and Q12

Q20. In the case of each of the following, please rank what you consider to be the degree of similarity between Irish and Chinese cultures.

Q12. For how long have you been doing business with China or Chinese people?

		a) More than 3 years	b) 12 months to 3 years	c) Less than 12 months	d) Have never done business with china	Response totals
a) Respects/obeys authority	Very Similar	3.9% (3)	0.0% (0)	0.0% (0)	0.0% (0)	
	Some Similarity	56.6% (43)	84.2% (16)	25.0% (1)	83.3% (5)	
	Little Similarity	39.5% (30)	15.8% (3)	75.0% (3)	16.7% (1)	
		76	19	4	6	105
e) Importance of saving face/avoiding losing face	Very Similar	6.5% (5)	0.0% (0)	0.0% (0)	0.0% (0)	
	Some Similarity	36.4% (28)	57.9% (11)	60.0% (3)	33.3% (2)	
	Little Similarity	57.1% (44)	42.1% (8)	40.0% (2)	66.7% (4)	
		77	19	5	6	107
f) Flexible in following regulations	Very Similar	11.8% (9)	15.8% (3)	0.0% (0)	0.0% (0)	
	Some Similarity	48.7% (37)	68.4% (13)	25.0% (1)	83.3% (5)	
	Little Similarity	39.5% (30)	15.8% (3)	75.0% (3)	16.7% (1)	
		76	19	4	6	105

53

in China more than three years, however, later appear to have readjusted their evaluation of similarity having become more knowledgeable about Chinese culture, coming to recognise that there were profound differences between the two cultures. Table 2 shows a move from 'little similarity' in the doing business in China for 'less than twelve months' group towards 'some similarity' in the 'twelve months to three years' group, and then back towards 'little similarity' in the 'more than three years group'. This implies that there is a long-term learning process, a deepening of understanding that comes with time, which also points to an appreciation over time of the reality that there are difficulties to be overcome and distances to be bridged in intercultural business relationships between Irish and Chinese people.

The Impact of Irish Cultural Tradition

By looking at Irish cultural tradition we can better understand the Irish perception of sharing some similarities with Chinese culture. In fact, there are parallels with Irish culture, if not exact comparisons. Irish culture, particularly rural culture, under the British Empire and under Anglo-Irish landlords, tended to obey rather than to respect authority, out of fear. The lack of rights to ownership of property, and the lack of control over one's own destiny, meant that one's face, i.e. one's social status or acceptance in the group, was more important. The pressures and enticements to 'go over to the other side' were intense, and led to extreme forms of face-related reactions in retaliation. During the famine in the nineteenth century people who converted to the Church of Ireland because of the enticement of Protestant soup kitchens were ostracised as 'soupers'. The term to 'boycott' a person came from a particularly brutal landlord's agent in the west of Ireland, Captain Boycott, who the local people refused to have anything to do with – socialise, serve in shops, etc. – as the only way they could deal with him.

The intent of British rule in Ireland, particularly under the Penal Laws, was to subjugate the people, replace Irish culture with English, and ban the practice of the Catholic religion, including by killing its priests. The Irish developed a suspicion of regulations, but also of British law and the judiciary, which were seen as a weapon of the Empire, and of the landlords. Because the Irish had a justifiable distrust of 'officialdom' they tended to rely on friends to get 'favours' and on influence, an Irish version of *guanxi*. In seeking a linguistic equivalent to *guanxi*, the term *ceangal* might fit; a word that means 'connection' in Irish.

Also, there would have been very few Irish who had the privilege of getting formal education, and virtually none would have become lawyers; consequently, there would have been suspicion about contracts and anything to do with the law. Like the Chinese, the Irish would be slow to trust strangers, until they got to know them. British spies and paid informers had been common in the past. While it is nearly a century since Irish independence, the fact that British rule lasted seven centuries means that its mark still remains in Irish culture.

INTERCULTURAL TRUST

In seeking to understand trust issues in the unique and complex Chinese context, it is worth considering different theoretical viewpoints in the academic literature on trust in business. It has been argued – from research done in British and German contexts for example – that trust-based relationships between buyer and supplier firms are socially constructed through a historical process in different countries and 'rarely evolve spontaneously on the level of individual interaction but are highly dependent on the existence of stable legal, political, and social institutions'.[20] In China, however, while institutional frameworks are unquestionably relevant, this research finds that so too are individual human relations in the way businesspeople in China create trust. Trust is also sometimes theorised as a 'rational choice', based on the idea of social actors as calculating, self-interested beings,[21] and such a view may seem particularly relevant to human behaviour in business. Building trust in China is clearly recognised as a rational necessity by most participants in this research, but this does not exclude the presence of genuine warmth and generosity in the human relationships involved. Other scholars have emphasised moral and altruistic norms of behaviour as the basis of trust,[22] and this study has certainly found that individuals doing business in China benefit by establishing themselves as trustworthy partners who can be relied on. What is widely agreed in the academic literature and by the findings of this research is that trust, howsoever it is theorised, is extremely important in business.

An overwhelmingly positive response was given by our respondents to the question, 'In your opinion, how important is intercultural trust for successfully doing business in or with China?', with 62 respondents out of 113 (54.9) viewing it as 'very important' and 41 out of 113 (36.3 per cent) viewing it as 'important' (see Chart 9).

The Trust Issue in the Particular Context of Chinese Business Culture

Trust is important in all business cultures, but it is particularly important in the context of Chinese business culture, as Chinese business to a great extent relies on personal relationships based on trust. As one of our interviewees suggested, 'for [the] Chinese, what you notice is that the business relationship is all based on trust and not on the contract as such' (LV9). Thus, intercultural trust in relation to personal communication and relationships is emphasised by Irish businesspeople:

> I think there still has to be trust and liking for one another to do business. I think if a Chinese person does not like you, he's not going to do business with you, even though you might have the best product in the world, if there's no relationship – and this is what it's all about, the trust, building the relationship. (LV11)

Many Irish companies and organisations attribute their business success to a reputation of trust they built up with the Chinese.

> We don't sell any product to anybody, unless they pay first. So, they pay 100 per cent first and then we send. So that, in China, was a lot of trust there. If a client gives us seventy thousand dollars this week, we have to deliver next Tuesday. We could walk away but I'm lucky that over the years, we've built up a reputation of trust with people. There are many companies out there that can sell the same product at the same price and they would approach some of our clients – competition – but our customers stick with us because of this trust. (VL12)

They learned to appreciate the friendship Chinese people offered to them and consider it to be the best way to create and maintain the trust between them.

> As far as I'm concerned, that [building up friendship]'s even more successful than doing the business deal because they've brought trust to you and you've brought trust to them and built up that relationship. So, hopefully, from there, you can go into even bigger things and better things, you know. (CL16)

The commonly expressed view that building trust with Chinese business partners by developing a good personal relationship was commonly accepted by Irish businesspeople and they reported often going out for dinner and drinking with their Chinese partners as a way to improve interpersonal trust:

> What it takes is some time to get to know people better, time in terms of out to dinner with people, drinking with them, they expect you to be a man.
>
> [Interviewer: What does that mean?]
>
> They will challenge you, drinking!
>
> [Interviewer: Create the trust, do they?]
>
> Yeah, it creates the relationship and it is the kind of thing that you need to do here if you are going to build any kind of a friendship in this who-knows-who environment. (F1)

Perhaps somewhat unexpectedly given common perceptions of the legal profession, a cooperative relationship between an Irish and a Chinese law firm was reported as built on trust, reinforcing its importance in the Chinese context:

> [Interviewer: The normal perception people have of this is 'where's the contract to sign' whereas you were saying ... you actually work on trust ... do you? You know, with the relationships that you have there.]
>
> Oh yes, that's right with firms in China. It's quite a complicated issue with law, the politics between law firms; law firms don't get married too easily, it's quite a big thing if a firm decides to say 'okay – myself and that firm over there we're tight now, we're going to –'. Basically what they're doing when they do that is they commit to exclusively refer work to each other .... It takes a while before you reach that stage. (CL17)

The same interviewee was keen to emphasise a practical approach of 'common sense' when dealing with Chinese businesspeople, and not to expect universal familiarity with Western norms.

Factors that Contribute to Building Successful Mutual Trust

The known Irish business cultural approach to building up mutual trust through personal relationships was reflected in the questionnaire survey responses. When asked, 'Which of the factors would contribute to building successful mutual trust between your company or organisation and your Chinese business partner(s) and/or your Chinese employees?', of 114 respondents, 58 (50.9 per cent) ticked 'personal connections', 55 (48.2 per cent) 'development of friendship' and 53 (46.5 per cent) 'inter-personal communication skills' (see Chart 10).

However, three other factors were even more important for building mutual trust between two business parties. The largest number, 70 respondents out of 114 (61.4 per cent), thought that 'cross-cultural knowledge/awareness' was a factor that 'would contribute to building successful mutual trust between (their) company or organisation and (their) Chinese business partner(s) and/or (their) Chinese employees' (see Chart 10). The other two most significant factors, with 68 respondents out of 114 (59.6 per cent) indicating them, were 'professional competence' and 'fulfilling promises' (see Chart 10).

One other factor that they deemed to be important was multi-language abilities (51.8 per cent). Given that the design of the questionnaire pre-selected a list of factors, the possibility remains that some other factors were omitted, but it seems significant how low support for 'ability to empathise' was (26.3 per cent) (see Chart 10).

PROBLEMS PREVENTING BUSINESSES ACHIEVING GREATER SUCCESS IN CHINA

Although most Irish businesspeople surveyed have developed a good knowledge of Chinese business culture and a body of experience in dealing with the cultural issues, there are still problems which prevent them from achieving greater success in China (see Chart 11).

Language Barrier

When asked 'which of the following problems are preventing you from achieving greater success in doing business in or with China', the greatest number, accounting for almost half of the respondents (46 per cent) selected 'language barrier' (see Chart 11). Moreover, when asked to rank in order the three most important factors from those they identified as problems, 13 respondents out of 98 (13.3 per cent) ranked 'language barrier' as 'most important', 14 out of 82 (17.1 per cent) as 'second in importance' and 9 out of 74 (12.2 per cent) as 'third in importance' (see Chart 12).

This result indicates that the language barrier is still an issue even though English is the common working language in Irish business dealings with China. Over the last decade or so in business studies, the relationship between language and management styles and culture has been increasingly recognised, as has the impact on intercultural business dealings of how far apart two languages are from each other. Linguistic distance from English predicts other important aspects of culture. For example, as distance from English increases, Hofstede's 'individualism' measure has been found to decrease, while 'power distance' increases.[23] Mandarin is known to be considerably distant from English,[24] and the implication is that this wide linguistic distance correlates with a wide cultural distance. Several key issues in relation to the language barrier were evident from the interviews:

- The quality of the interpreter
- The accuracy of the written translation
- Lack of knowledge of the language impeding a deeper understanding of Chinese culture

Quality of the Interpreter

The Irish businesspeople interviewed indicated that not all interpreters provide a high-quality service. Some Chinese interpreters have a tendency to cushion what is being said from the Irish business side:

> So you might have been angry or you might have been extremely concerned trying to say something and the interpreter would tone it down.

> [Interviewer: Would re-interpret it?]

> Yeah, yeah. And, like I say, there were some who were better at being reliable and people that you could truly trust to say, tell them that I said exactly this, and also tell me exactly what they said. (F1)

Accuracy of the Written Translation

The language barrier can be a serious issue for some Irish businesspeople whose communication with their Chinese business partner heavily relies on written correspondence. In these situations accurate translations are essential, and any error can cause misunderstanding and result in business failure. When asked what were the major obstacles he had encountered throughout the years that he had spent in China, one interviewee replied:

> I suppose language in a way, and interpretation of your language, and dealing with China; a lot of my direct dealings, if I wasn't in situ with the suppliers or manufacturers or trading houses, if I wasn't on site with them, 90 per cent of my communication was by the medium of telex, in the earliest days, and by fax thereafter. So your written correspondence, you had to use particularly straightforward English with no grey areas, it was very black and white, so it couldn't be misinterpreted or misconstrued. The importance of effective written communication could not be overstressed. (H5)

Lack of Knowledge of the Language Impeding a Deeper Understanding of Chinese Culture

The experience of being able to do business in China without learning much of the Chinese language has acted as a disincentive to Irish business-people to make a commitment to overcome all difficulties and fully grasp Chinese language skills. Most of them have only learned the minimum for basic conversation – just enough for them to survive in a socioculturally different environment.

> They can be a little bit lazy, in that the Chinese people that they will mix with will usually be able to speak English pretty well. So, they will just learn a hundred words and they will use those same one hundred words while they are in China and they will not learn anything more than that – just a hundred words, to be able to get around, to go to places, to get home, supermarkets, etcetera. So, that's how they deal with it. (LV9)

Language is naturally itself part of a culture and knowledge of it illuminates and helps cultural understanding. Thus, many of the Irish businesspeople surveyed have realised that their lack of skills in the Chinese language can prevent them from appreciating the rich culture of China:

> So it is up to us, if we want to make this effort initially at overcoming this language barrier so that we can communicate efficiently with

these people and try and learn a tiny part of what they have to offer, and I think that is the most humbling thing, to be able to be in a position to do something like that, because I see so many people who maybe don't have this chance, or don't realise that this richness [of Chinese culture] exists. (F3)

Therefore, the lack of language ability in communicating in Chinese is thought to be a disadvantage in doing business in China, particularly for those who are junior or new to the Chinese market, and who have an urgent need to build up a network of personal connections. The survey revealed that the percentage of respondents who regarded the 'language barrier' as a problem decreased as the length of time of their doing business with China increased, with 83.3 per cent seeing it as a problem among those who have not done business with China yet, 60 per cent among those with less than twelve months' experience in China, 50 per cent of those with between twelve months' and three years' experience, and 39.7 per cent among those who have more than three years' experience

Issues with Chinese Regulations

When asked, 'Which of the following problems are preventing you from achieving greater success in doing business in or with China?', 44 respondents out of 100 (44 per cent) ticked 'Chinese regulations' (see Chart 11). This represented the other most significant factor along with 'language barrier'. And when asked, 'What kind of information is essential for doing business in China?', 54.6 per cent and 51.9 per cent respectively responded 'about Chinese government policies' and 'about the Chinese legal system and business law' (see Chart 13). These factors combined indicate that getting to know the Chinese business environment from a political and legal perspective is a constant challenge for Irish companies and organisations; this applies even to those business-people who are relatively mature in the market.

Specific problems concerning Chinese regulations identified in the interviews were:

1. Dealing with Chinese regulations and laws in a framework of bureaucracy and corruption was found to be a serious barrier to achieving business success in China. For example, corruption in

the Chinese Customs Office impeded a seafood import/export company and resulted in serious financial loss:

> They look at our documents and if a 'T' doesn't have a cross, or an 'I' doesn't have a dot – it's not coming into China. You could lose fifty, sixty, seventy, eighty thousand dollars .... (LV12)

2. Some of the newly issued Chinese regulations and laws are different in purpose and philosophy from those practised in Western countries. For example, some Chinese regulations and laws do not serve to increase fair competition. They may be intended to strengthen governmental control over a market or to give some companies an unfair advantage:

> One of the challenges is the regulation, the government control of these things, and the fact that local companies like [Company D] are guaranteed a certain percentage of the market, and also the actual telecom operators are forced to support local standards as well, as in TDS-CDMA, which is a Chinese-developed mobile standard. They have to support this also, and this gives local manufacturers like [Company E] an advantage, an unfair advantage, as would be seen by companies like [Company A] and [Company B], that they have an advantage, that they automatically get a certain percent[age] of the market. (H3)

3. Sometimes an Irish company or organisation may have to deal with perceived inconsistency and contradiction in the regulations:

> [Rules about] importing raw materials [are] very stringent. Sometimes [they] can have illogical and nonsensical Chinese regulations around importing goods and labelling and documentation; and things can frequently get held up in Customs when they are doing their inspections for a couple of weeks, which can delay your production, which obviously affects your reputation. (H4)

4. As discussed earlier, Chinese principles and approaches to following rules differ from the Irish approach. Chinese flexibility about

following rules can sometimes cause problems for Irish business dealings with China.

Miscommunication

As the third most significant barrier preventing respondents 'from achieving greater success in doing business in or with China', 33 respondents out of 100 (33 per cent) identified miscommunication (see Chart 11). Interviews helped provide deeper information on the main reasons for this problem, as set out below:

- Cultural differences
- Lack of language skills

Cultural Differences

In their business dealings with China, Irish businesspeople experienced a cultural gap and distance which could cause miscommunication. The following is an example of a face-related indirectness that blocked communication between two parties:

> Some of the [Chinese] girls will get really sad if you are annoyed with them, you know; and you're not angry with them, you just maybe want a different answer, or you want them to work a bit harder or you want them to do something different, and they get all upset, or they won't speak to you for days and you're like, oh my God, this has to be professional. You can't explain that that wasn't personal .... (CL13)

Similarly, it was advised that a foreign business representative should not express a negative opinion straightaway in a negotiation, because this would embarrass the Chinese party and could end the relationship, destroying any chance of business cooperation:

> If the Chinese party proposes something that is totally unacceptable to the foreign party, you can't say that. You can't say, 'That's totally unacceptable.' (LV9)

Moreover, detailed arrangements for conducting meetings with Chinese businesspeople need to be carefully considered, otherwise communication channels can be blocked:

Even the way the people sit at the table is structured and the method for greeting people is different. Who is conducting the negotiations is often very important – who's asking the questions and who's responding? You can't be asking questions all the time – you have to be equal. The other side has to be able to ask their questions. (LV9)

Lack of Language Skills

Apart from the cultural knowledge discussed above, the language barrier is an obvious factor that can cause problems of miscommunication:

For a multinational having to deal with phone conferences would be a major challenge [where] … I think a lot of miscommunications occur, and people saying 'yes' when maybe they don't really understand; this can lead to some tricky situations in projects, things not being completed. I think you need a person on the ground; telephone conferences and things like that will not get the job done, you have to actually be there as well, to have a physical presence on the management on site. (H3)

Difficulties with Mutual Trust

Some businesspeople surveyed confidently suggested that it is not difficult to build trust with Chinese business partners.

I think people are very open and relaxed. I think there's still some way to go, on the rule of law – everyone accepts that – but still, it's a lot easier to do business here …. So, I think trust isn't really a problem. (LV10)

However, many others experienced difficulties with establishing and maintaining a relationship of trust. Corruption was identified as one of the major problems that prevent Irish companies and organisations from trusting their Chinese business partners:

I think the experience a lot of companies have over there with corruption and things like this, trust is a very hard thing to build. The relationship has to be ongoing for a while before you would say that there is trust within the relationship. I think the fear of being asked for backhanders or things like this is a very real fear on the part of the Western side of the relationship, and this is something that is maybe very hard for them to swallow. (H3)

The other problem is that some Chinese partners are dishonest in their business dealings with Westerners:

They will substitute poor material, they will show you one level of quality and get you to buy off and accept that that is what you are going to get from them, and then they turn out to be substituting components and doing things that make quality not as good; and it is really, really important to put measures and checkpoints and controls in place. (F1)

Some Chinese partners may take advantage of their language ability, local knowledge and personal connections and thereby try to take over or duplicate a business:

I have seen a lot of situations here where Chinese have partnered with foreigners and have either successfully or attempted to gain control and hurt the foreigners that have been dealing with them. They take advantage of their language capabilities and their friendship capabilities and things that the foreigners maybe are not so experienced with here; and they are very quick to copy what someone is doing and subsequently take it on their own so they could duplicate it. Once they have the opportunity to go and learn and see what someone is doing, they can duplicate it very quickly and set something up with their who-knows-who relationships to in effect take over that business or take it away from a foreigner. (F1)

Moreover, the distrust is a two-way issue and Chinese businesspeople do not automatically trust their Western business partners either. They are suspicious and cautious, taking time to have the confidence to trust their business partners:

I guess one of the things I would say about the friendships is that they start off very superficially because they also don't trust you. (F1)

Information Scarcity

When asked what problems are preventing them from achieving greater success in doing business in or with China, 29 respondents out of the 100 who replied to this question ticked 'information scarcity' (see Chart 10). Among these 29 per cent of respondents, more than half did not have a physical business presence in China. This sheds light on a likely reason for their problem with information scarcity. China's fast-growing economy and rapidly expanding market requires Irish companies and organisations to collect up-to-date information on a daily basis, otherwise crucial information could be easily missed – not only by a company or by an organisation, but even by a whole market sector.

> So, Ireland needs to focus on the service sector. That's where Europe has arrived – in the services sector – but now, China wants to get into that area and to dominate that area; you know, the capital market in China has taken off in the last ten years. So, I'm amazed that the large service providers in Ireland – and in other countries, but especially in Ireland – that they haven't set up services operations in China. At least, that they haven't set up rep offices to be the eyes and ears of their business in China, to let them know what's happening and what's going on, you know. (LV9)

This is a good example of the danger that the Irish economy will be left behind if sufficient representative offices are not set up in China. Representative offices as the 'eyes and ears of their business in China' have to be regarded as absolutely crucial for Irish companies and organisations to achieve business success. However, many Irish companies and organisations have not so far been aware of their importance and the possibilities they could generate:

> Now, maybe Enterprise Ireland can help them and can give them information; but I think that, in addition to that information from Enterprise Ireland, they should focus on, you know, perhaps setting up a representative office in China, which is very cheap to set up. Most people in Ireland – businesspeople – don't know you can set up a representative office. (LV9)

Lack of Personal Relationships

To the question, 'Which of the following problems are preventing you from achieving greater success in doing business in or with China?', the sixth most recognised factor, identified by 26 per cent of the respondents, was 'lack of personal relationships' (see Chart 11). This suggests that although most Irish companies and organisations surveyed are coping well, it should be noted that they still need more support in establishing personal connections in China. More than half of the respondents, 61 out of 108 (56.5 per cent), selected 'information to help establish personal connections' when asked 'What kind of information is essential for doing business in China?' (see Chart 11).

Chapter 5

Demand for Chinese Expertise and Training Programmes

DEMAND

A heavy demand among Irish companies and organisations for Chinese expertise and training programmes in the Chinese language, culture and business culture has been found throughout our survey.

Among the Irish businesspeople surveyed, only 37.9 per cent of respondents claimed that they had participated in previous training (61.4 per cent of these in language, 61.4 per cent in Chinese culture and 56.8 per cent in doing business with China), while 61.4 per cent of respondents had not received any such training whatsoever. This particular data points to a major and increasing gap for Irish higher education to fill. As one businessman indicated in his interview:

> A lot of Western organisations only start thinking about these things when they are already in China ... they don't prepare before they go .... Also, cultural awareness of China and knowledge of the workings of China is *not* an on-going thing in Irish companies. Obvious things like language, interacting with Chinese students in Ireland, cultural exchange with the Western company, preparing companies for the challenges that other companies have seen and overcome ...would be beneficial. Experiences could be shared through the institute or university. (D3H)

Another businessman stressed the importance of knowing another culture and the role of education in bridging the gap between Irish and Chinese culture:

> Knowledge of another culture is fundamental ... the history of China, particularly the last 150 to 200 years, is very important in terms of understanding. Education is key'. (D1H)

To help identify types of Chinese expertise and training programmes requested by Irish companies and organisations, two questions were designed in the questionnaire. One question asked, 'What kinds of university graduates do you think would be suitable to help your company/organisation to develop business links with China?' More than three-quarters, 78.4 per cent, of respondents responded positively to 'Bachelor of Commerce with Chinese Studies', 48.5 per cent to 'Master of Science in Chinese Business Studies' and 16.5 per cent to 'Bachelor of Arts in Chinese Studies' (see Chart 14).

The other question asked was, 'What is a good way for you or your employees to acquire the training/skills' required and to this question 52 per cent of respondents registered interest in 'intensive short-term courses (three days, five days, ten days, etc.)' and 40.2 per cent in 'evening courses in Chinese-related studies'. These were followed by significant demand for 'part-time degree in Chinese language and culture', a 'study tour of China' and 'online distance learning', by 27.5 per cent, 25.5 per cent and 24.5 per cent of respondents respectively. Around one-fifth of respondents showed interest in an MBA training programme: 21.6 per cent of respondents gave a positive response to 'Chinese-focused MBA programme with summer tour in China' and 19.6 per cent to 'Chinese-focused MBA programme' (see Chart 15).

A majority of Irish businesspeople prioritised training in Chinese business culture and to the question, 'From a cultural perspective which of the following might help your company/organisation to achieve greater success in doing business in or with China?', 61 out of 111 respondents (55 per cent) selected 'study Chinese business culture'. As for training in the Chinese language and Chinese culture in general, more Irish businesspeople surveyed preferred to 'study Chinese culture and language combined', with 53 of 111 respondents (47.7 per cent) respond-ing positively. Around one-quarter of respondents (28 and 26 out of 111, 25.2 per cent and 23.4 per cent) gave positive responses to 'study Chinese culture' and 'study Chinese language' respectively (see Chart 16).

Regarding training in Chinese business culture, information 'about Chinese business practices' was viewed by the Irish businesspeople surve-yed as overwhelmingly important: 95 out of 108 respondents (88 per cent) chose this item (see Chart 13). As one of our interviewees suggested:

> If the course was run by people who had first-hand experience [in China] rather than just researching and regurgitating it … a

one-day course would be beneficial if done in the right way and given by somebody who had first-hand experience of living and working in China. (K1H)

Apart from business practice information, other information in relation to Chinese business culture was also highlighted, with 63 per cent of respondents giving a positive response to information 'about Chinese culture and customs', 56.5 per cent to 'information to help establish personal connections', 54.6 per cent to information 'about Chinese government policies' and 51.9 per cent to 'information about the Chinese legal system and business law' (see Chart 13).

This data provides clarity and direction about what should be focused on when running a degree programme or a training programme in Chinese business culture. The following five topics, deemed by respondents to be 'essential', should be included and fully explored in all programmes:

- Chinese business practice
- Chinese culture and customs
- Information to help establish connections
- China's government policies
- The Chinese legal system and business law

Moreover, our interview data has provided valuable information in addition to that collected from the questionnaire survey. Various forms and flexible arrangements of training programmes were suggested:

Intercultural training, morning seminars in universities … seminars within companies, intercultural training for people who will be interacting with China … to help get the best out of their business dealings with China. (D1H)

If there was a half-day seminar on the workings of the Chinese government, everything the businessman needs to know … I would be there; or of the Chinese financial system, ministry of education or … ministry of trade or political affairs. That would be extremely interesting. (D2H)

For Irish organisations like a university, special training programmes were recommended through which all staff in direct contact with

Chinese students would be trained and voluntary information would be provided:

> To increase understanding of China, its markets and its peoples … just information, seminars, festivals, the subtle work of introducing Chinese food or Chinese cultural events into the calendar of the year … and more overtly, having [a] half-day, one-hour, half-hour lunchtime session on Chinese cultural norms … people would find that interesting and sign up for it …. Maybe a case for tailormade short courses or seminars to people who will be engaged like the admissions office, the accommodation office, catering office, etc. … almost a compulsory course for people in direct contact [with Chinese students or Chinese academics] and then voluntary information sessions for people who have an interest. (D2H)

Based on the evidence from both the questionnaire and the interview survey, the UCD Confucius Institute for Ireland piloted and ran training programmes for Irish companies and organisations in the first half of 2009, details of which are discussed below.

DESIGN OF TRAINING PROGRAMMES

Having conducted research into the extent and types of demand that exist in Ireland for training in Chinese business expertise, the UCD Confucius Institute for Ireland has identified a range of course types to meet the various needs of several target groups within the country. The content of these courses varies according to the needs and requirements of their respective audiences, but all are based on expert knowledge of China and its language and culture, with particular reference to building and maintaining successful and mutually beneficial business relationships between Irish and Chinese people. The design of the courses is informed by both primary and secondary research and aims to provide relevant and up-to-date training of the highest possible quality. It is envisaged that significant numbers of Irish business students and practitioners will participate and that knowledge and appreciation of China, with better expertise in forging win–win relationships between the two countries, will be well served by implementing these programmes. The quality and continued value of these courses is maintained through strong built-in quality assurance and update features. Training programmes are as follows:

- Doing Business in China: intensive programme 1 (half-day)
- Doing Business in China: intensive programme 2 (two half-days)
- Understanding China: in-company corporate training programme
- Certificate in Chinese Business and Culture (intensive one-week programme in China with a partner university)
- Chinese Business and Culture Workshop (partnership programme with the Ireland China Association, the Dublin Chamber of Commerce or Chambers Ireland, etc.)
- Chinese Business and Practices (two-week summer programme)
- Diploma in Chinese Business and Culture (two-hour sessions, fifteen-week programme)
- Chinese Language and Business (one evening a week, fifteen-week programme)
- Chinese Language and Culture (one evening a week, fifteen-week programme)

Chapter 6

Pilot Training Programmes

CASE STUDY 1 – TRAINING FOR SENIOR EXECUTIVES FROM CRH GROUP

In May 2009, the UCD Confucius Institute for Ireland delivered a one-day bespoke training programme on Chinese business and culture for senior executives from CRH Group, the Irish Fortune 500 multinational building materials and construction services company whose global operations include major investment in China.

The programme covered a diverse range of specialist topics, including an Ireland–China briefing, Chinese society and economy, the business environment, the legal system, history, Confucian philosophy, customer service management, press and media, research and innovation, calligraphy and insights into doing business in the north-east of the country.

The programme was intensive and interactive, with in-depth discussions on many aspects and points. Up-to-date findings from the Confucius Institute's national survey of Irish companies and organisations on the need for support and expertise in Chinese business and training helped inform the design of those presentations specifically aimed at Irish business management individuals seeking a better understanding of and insight into China. This training course represents an initiative of considerable significance and potential, reflects current global trends, and was among the first of its kind in Ireland. The cooperation between a major Irish business organisation and academic expertise in Ireland is very promising in terms of improving future business and economic links between Ireland and China.

The five participating executives from CRH Group gave full recognition and credit to the format and content of the training course. One of CRH's business representatives in China said:

> I really appreciate that the Confucius Institute and Ireland China Association could offer such a high quality and tailormade course

to us. The programme was great and the time flew by very quickly. I'm very fond of Harbin in China, because the people there are very friendly.

Another businessman at senior management level in the company commented:

The key to conducting business is good communication between people, so learning about Chinese culture is very important to us. We can only better develop and extend our business in China if we can fully understand and appreciate Chinese people and their culture.

The executive training programme for CRH has attracted the interest of other Irish firms keen on investing in China, and several other multi-national companies are negotiating with UCD's Confucius Institute for Ireland to develop similar courses.

CASE STUDY 2 – TWELVE-WEEK COURSE IN CHINESE LANGUAGE, BUSINESS AND CULTURE

Based on popular demand from the members of the Ireland China Association (ICA) (www.irelandchina.org), as well as the previous success of a similar executive training programme in 2008 on Chinese language, business and culture, the UCD Confucius Institute for Ireland partnered with the ICA in March 2009 to deliver a twelve-week-long programme targeted primarily at ICA members as well as business executives/entrepreneurs who are doing business with China at either market entry or intermediate level stage.

Following on from the approval of the programme design proposal in March by an ICA council meeting, the UCD Confucius Institute for Ireland officially launched its programme under the title 'Understanding China, Navigating Dynamics – Chinese Language, Culture and Business Executive Programme'. The twelve-week course was offered at two locations (Merrion Square and the UCD Quinn School of Business), with a choice of dates each week (either Tuesday or Thursday).

The basis of the programme was fundamentally an intensive Mandarin Chinese language course (beginners' level) with the option of a wide range of elective seminars or public lectures. Ten speakers were invited to deliver talks on separate topics based on their expertise on and/or experience of China. The programme aimed to offer the participants an elaborative learning opportunity about China from political, legal, sociocultural, historical and economic/business perspectives. After successful completion of the programme, participants were expected to have acquired elementary levels of Chinese language skills and knowledge about interacting within a Chinese environment, as well as essential business skills for immediate application to transactions with China.

The programme commenced on 21 April 2009, and was successfully completed on 9 July 2009. Participants joined the programme from various organisations and sectors: Fortune Global 500 companies, Irish government agencies, chambers of commerce, active entrepreneurs and executive MBA students from both UCD and Trinity business schools. Industry backgrounds ranged from IT, healthcare and marketing, to R&D, investment banking and the civil service.

The official graduation ceremony was held on 7 July 2009, when all participants received a certificate jointly conferred by the CII and the ICA. An evening reception drew the programme to an official close.

The decision to limit the length of the programme to twelve weeks was due to: 1) feedback from previous Chinese language learners (beginners' level) that a fifteen- or twenty-week programme involves too much of a time commitment, particularly for business executives, and 2) the holiday season in July and August, with the twelve-week duration starting in April allowing completion by early July.

By offering two locations, the programme was unique compared with all other Chinese language schools in Dublin, being able to provide flexibility to participants who may have missed the first session of the week, by repeating it on an alternative day in the same week.

Chapter 7

Conclusions and Recommendations

B ased on the results of this survey research, the main cultural issues Irish companies and organisations are facing in doing business in China are as follows:

1. Irish companies and organisations need to be properly prepared before entering the Chinese market by further improving their awareness of the importance of understanding Chinese language, culture and business practices. This is clearly demonstrated as essential for Irish businesses to achieve greater success in the most tantalising and dynamic emerging market in the world.

2. Lack of language ability in communicating in Chinese and lack of understanding of Chinese culture are major barriers to or disadvantages in doing business in China, particularly for those who are new to the Chinese market or have an urgent need to build up a network of personal connections. For the sake of competitive advantage in doing business in China, language fluency and cultural fluency are essential.

3. Getting to know the Chinese market from a political and legal perspective is a constant challenge for Irish companies and organisations. China's rapidly expanding economy and fast-changing markets have been accompanied by many new government policies, laws and regulations. Dealing with the Chinese government's policies, laws and regulations in a framework of bureaucracy and corruption is found to be a serious barrier that can prevent Irish businesses from achieving success in China. Moreover, one of the dynamics of Chinese business is that, in some cases, there are no fixed rules and regulations. Therefore, understanding the flexibility of Chinese people towards implementing regulations and laws

is even more important than understanding the regulations and laws themselves.

4. Building intercultural trust in a Chinese business environment is very challenging for Irish companies and organisations, but it is a key factor in successful business relationships. Corruption is found to have prevented Irish companies and organisations from establishing and maintaining trust-based relationships with their Chinese business partners. In extreme cases, there exists a risk of dishonesty among Chinese partners and this may lead to serious damage or failure of Irish businesses in China.

5. China's fast-growing economy and dynamic emerging market require Irish companies and organisations to collect up-to-date information on a daily basis; otherwise, crucial information could be easily missed – not only by a company or by an organisation, but even by a whole market sector.

6. Many Irish companies and organisations need support to help establish personal connections in China, although many of them have already realised the crucial role which personal connections play in doing business in China and are making considerable efforts in this regard.

7. Compared with other European cultures and American culture, Irish culture shares more similarities with Chinese culture. Awareness and understanding of the similarities has been found to be beneficial to Irish companies and organisations in adapting to the Chinese market and developing long-term trading links with China.

In response to the cultural issues listed above, we put forward the following recommendations:

1. The current economic recession has provided Irish companies and organisations with an added incentive to develop new market strategies and to give more weight to Asian markets, especially the rapidly expanding Chinese market.

2. The Irish government and its agents should give further support to the Irish higher education system to develop degree programmes to meet the urgent need of Irish companies and organisations for Chinese expertise, such as undergraduate and postgraduate programmes that combine Chinese with the study of business, law

or politics. Training courses offering expertise in Chinese language, culture and business practices are also an important source of knowledge on China and should be urgently provided.

3. Sufficient and up-to-date information on China and the Chinese market should be made readily available to Irish companies and organisations. Such information includes information on Chinese culture and customs, Chinese business practices, Chinese government policies and regulations, the Chinese legal system and business law, as well as information to help establish personal connections.

4. Establishing representative offices in China has proven to be one of the best ways to receive up-to-date information regarding the Chinese market. More support should be given to Irish companies and organisations to establish such local offices, such as providing crucial information regarding their staff requirements, venues, protocols and the associated set-up and running costs.

5. A database of Chinese alumni should be established to help Irish companies and organisations find qualified Chinese employees both in Ireland and in China. This database should primarily contain information about Chinese alumni who, through their experience in living and studying in both China and Ireland, have developed a good understanding of both cultures, are fluent in both Chinese and English and are capable of helping to establish personal connections in China.

6. Irish businesspeople entering the Chinese business environment should be aware that Irish social and business networks exist in China, which may offer opportunities to make personal connections and obtain information useful to their business dealings.

7. Irish businesspeople embarking on doing business in China should first look to the possibilities the Chinese in Ireland may have to offer.

Endnotes

[1] Huang, Y. and Sterquist, B. (2007), 'Retailers' Foreign Market Entry Decisions: An Institutional Perspective', *International Business Review*, Vol. 16, No. 5, pp. 613–629.

[2] Chapman, J.C. and Xu, W. (2008), 'The Road to China: Ten Key Lessons on Doing Business in China', *Nixon Peabody LLP*, 25 February 2008, available at: http://www.nixonpeabody.com/linked_media/publications/doing-business-in-china.pdf, Date of retrieval: 6 August 2009.

[3] Strange, R. (ed.) (1998), *Management in China: The Experience of Foreign Businesses*, London: Frank Cass Publishers.

[4] Zhang, T. (2007), 'Doing Business in China: Opportunities and Challenges for European Companies', *China Business Solutions*, May 2007, available at: http://www.chinabusinesssolutions.com/dbimg/doing_business_in_china__opportunities_and_challenges_for_european_companies_2007.pdf, Date of retrieval: 6 August 2009.

[5] Enterprise Ireland (2005), 'Doing Business in China, A Guide for Irish Companies', *Enterprise Ireland*, 2 November 2005, available from: http://www.enterprise-ireland.com/NR/rdonlyres/CE042179-5C62-441A-8362-08F4D64BFC1C/0/DoingBusinessinChina.pdf, Date of retrieval: 16 March 2010.

[6] Randelsome, C. and Myers, A. (1997), 'Cultural Fluency: Results from a UK and Ireland Survey', *Business Communication Quarterly*, Vol. 60, No. 3, pp. 9–22, p. 14.

[7] Randelsome and Myers (1997), 'Cultural Fluency', p. 21.

[8] Taylor, J. (2002), 'The China Context: A Study of Doing Business in China', Masters thesis (UCD Smurfit School of Business).

[9] Trampedach, S. (2002), 'Establishing a Business in China', Masters thesis (UCD Smurfit School of Business).

[10] Li, W. (2002), 'Entry Strategies of Irish Information Technology and Telecoms Companies into China Market', Masters thesis (UCD Smurfit School of Business).

[11] Corless, K. (2004), 'A Perspective on Inter-Cultural Business Negotiations: China', Masters thesis (UCD Smurfit School of Business).

[12] Keane, H. (2007), 'Climbing the Great Walls of China: The Challenges that Irish Projects Must Overcome in Order to Succeed in the Chinese Market', Masters thesis (UCD Smurfit School of Business).

13 O'Broin, S. and McQuillan, L. (2007), 'Scaling the Chinese Wall: Managerial Challenges Involved in Trading with China – An Irish Perspective', Masters thesis (UCD Smurfit School of Business).

14 Goggin, L. (2004), 'Perceptions, Influences and Consequences of Guanxi for Western Organizations Doing Business in China', Masters thesis (UCD Smurfit School of Business).

15 Zinzius, B. (2004), *Doing Business in the New China*, London: Praeger, p.144.

16 Interview F5.

17 Irish EU Minister Dick Roche quoted in *Time* magazine, 16 March 2008, on the occasion of Beijing's first ever Saint Patrick's Day parade. *Time* also reported that 'the event may be the first parade organized and led by foreigners in the Chinese capital in at least 50 years.' See http://www.time.com/time/world/article/0,8599,1722799,00.html, Date of retrieval: 16 March 2010.

18 Interview F4.

19 Kehoe, I. (2005), 'Family Values Dominate Irish Business', *Sunday Business Post*, 27 February 2005.

20 Lane, C. and Bachmann, R. (1996), 'The Social Constitution of Trust: Supplier Relations in Britain and Germany', *Organization Studies*, Vol. 17, No. 3, pp. 365–395, p. 365.

21 Coleman, J. (1990), *Foundations of Social Theory*, Cambridge, MA: Harvard University Press.

22 For example, Sako, M. (1992), *Prices, Quality and Trust: Inter-Firm Relations in Britain and Japan*, Cambridge: Cambridge University Press.

23 Graham, J.L. (2001), 'Culture and Human Resources Management', in A. Rugman and T.L. Brewer (eds.), *The Oxford Handbook of International Business*, Oxford University Press. See also Zinzius (2004), *Doing Business in the New China*.

24 Chiswick, B.R. and Miller, P. (2005), 'Linguistic Distance: A Quantitative Measure of the Distance between English and Other Languages', *Journal of Multilingual and Multicultural Development*, Vol. 26, No. 1, pp.1–11.

Appendix A

Questionnaire

We would like your assistance in completing this questionnaire to help us identify the cultural barriers facing Irish companies and organisations when doing business in or with China and to examine how Ireland's higher education can best address these problems and so meet the new demands of Irish companies and organisations in the rapidly changing world of the twenty-first century. Your responses will help to improve the environment involving Irish companies and firms dealing with their Chinese business partners. All the responses will remain anonymous and confidential.

Part One: About Yourself

Q1. Your age.

a) <25 [ ]   b) 25–35 [ ]   c) 35–45 [ ]   d) 45–55 [ ]   e) >55 [ ]

Q2. Your gender:

a) Male [ ]   b) Female [ ]

Q3. Are you:

a) Irish   [ ]   b) Western European/not Irish [ ]
c) Northern American   [ ]   d) Mainland Chinese   [ ]
e) Other Chinese   [ ]   f) Other   [ ]

Q4. Your position in your company/organisation:

a) Owner/director/senior management   [ ]
b) Middle management   [ ]
c) Junior management/executive   [ ]
d) Other (please specify) _____

Part Two: About Your Company/Organisation

Q5. How many people are employed in your company/organisation?

a) Fewer than 10 [ ]   b) 10–150 [ ]   c) more than 150 [ ]

Q6. Which of the following categories would best describe your business?

a) Manufacturing   [ ]
b) Marketing/retail   [ ]
c) Service/education   [ ]
d) Import/export   [ ]
e) Other (please specify) _____

Q7. What percentage of your revenue was based on the Chinese market during the last three years?

a) Below 1% [ ]   b) More than 1% but less than 10% [ ] c) Over 35% [ ]

Q8. Has your company/organisation employed Chinese people in the past three years?

a) Yes [ ]   b) No [ ]

Q9. If your answer to Q8 is 'Yes' please tell us how long you have had Chinese employees in your company/organisation?

a) Less than 1 year [ ]   b) 1 to 3 years [ ]   c) More than 3 years [ ]

Q10. Does your company/organisation have a physical business presence in China?

a) Yes [ ]   b) No [ ]

Q11. Does your company/organisation have a business partner or representatives in China?

a) Yes [ ]   b) No [ ]

Q12. For how long have you been doing business with China or Chinese people?

a) More than 3 years   [ ]
b) 12 months to 3 years   [ ]
c) Less than 12 months   [ ]
d) Have never done business with China   [ ]

Q13. How do you perceive your business involvement in China in the next five years?

a) Stop doing business in China   [ ]
b) Do less business in China   [ ]
c) No change   [ ]
d) Start doing business in China   [ ]
e) Do increased business in China   [ ]

Part Three: Cultural Issues

Q14. In your opinion, how important is "an awareness of cultural factors" for a company/organisation to have success in dealing with Chinese companies?

a) Very important   [   ]   b) Important   [   ]   c) Do not know   [   ]

d) Unimportant   [   ]   e) Irrelevant   [   ]

Q15. Which of the following factors do you think have contributed/will contribute to your success in your business dealings with China? (Please mark each alternative with an X, or else ignore.)

a) Language ability   [   ]   b) Communication skills   [   ]

c) Cultural knowledge   [   ]   d) Competent interpreters   [   ]

e) Access to information sources   [   ]   f) Understanding of the Chinese market   [   ]

g) Sufficient information   [   ]   h) Help from the Irish government   [   ]

i) Good personal relationships   [   ]   j) Irish government's policies   [   ]

k) Expertise in Chinese business   [   ]   l) Chinese government's policies   [   ]

m) Others (please specify) _____

Q16. Please rank, in order, the three most important factors from those you have listed in Q15 above:

a) Most important _____   b) Second in importance _____

c) Third in importance _____

Q17. Has your company/organisation participated in training in Chinese language or culture?

a) Yes   [   ]   b) No   [   ]

Q18. If the answer to Q17 is 'Yes' please indicate what kind of training your company/organisation has provided:

a) Chinese language   [   ]

b) Chinese culture   [   ]

c) Doing business in/with China   [   ]

d) Other (please specify) _____

Q19. Do you think Chinese culture shares more similarities with Irish culture than it does with other European cultures or with American culture?

a) Strongly agree   [   ]   b) Agree   [   ]   c) Do not know   [   ]

d) Disagree   [   ]   e) Strongly disagree   [   ]

Q20. In the case of each of the following, please rank what you consider to be the degree of similarity between Irish and Chinese cultures:

Categories	Very Similar	Some Similarity	Little Similarity
a) Respects/obeys authority	[ ]	[ ]	[ ]
b) Focus on family values	[ ]	[ ]	[ ]

Categories	Very Similar	Some Similarity	Little Similarity
c) Do business through personal connections	[ ]	[ ]	[ ]
d) Use long-term relationships to establish mutual trust	[ ]	[ ]	[ ]
e) Importance of saving face/avoiding losing face	[ ]	[ ]	[ ]
f) Flexible in following regulations	[ ]	[ ]	[ ]
g) Highly values friendship	[ ]	[ ]	[ ]
h) Community-centred	[ ]	[ ]	[ ]
i) In doing business, trusts family/kin more than non-family management/employees	[ ]	[ ]	[ ]
j) Other (please specify) _____			

Q21. Which of the following problems are preventing you from achieving greater success in doing business in/with China? (Please mark each alternative with an X, or else ignore.)

a) Language barrier   [ ]   b) Difficulty with mutual trust   [ ]
c) Cultural strangeness   [ ]   d) Lack of understanding of China   [ ]
e) Lack of Chinese business expertise   [ ]   f) Miscommunication   [ ]
     h) Lack of help from the Irish government   [ ]
g) Information scarcity   [ ]
i) Lack of personal relationships   [ ]   j) Chinese regulations   [ ]
k) Lack of knowledge of Chinese business culture   [ ]   l) Other (please specify) _____

Q22. Please rank, in order, the three most important factors from those you have listed in Q21 above:

a) Most important _____   b) Second in importance _____
c) Third in importance _____

Part Four: Intercultural Trust

Q23. In your opinion, how important is intercultural trust for successfully doing business in/with China?

a) Very important [ ]   b) Important [ ]   c) Do not know [ ]
d) Unimportant   [ ]   e) Irrelevant [ ]

Q24. In your opinion, which of the following factors would contribute to building successful mutual trust between your company/organisation and your Chinese business partner(s) and/or your Chinese employees? (Please mark each alternative with an X, or else ignore.)

a) Multi-language abilities   [ ]   b) Ability to empathise   [ ]
c) Cross-cultural knowledge/ awareness   [ ]   d) Inter-personal communication skills   [ ]

e) Professional competence   [ ]   f)   Personal connections   [ ]

g) Development of friendship   [ ]   h)   Fulfilling promises   [ ]

i)   Other (please specify) _____

Part Five: Demand for Expertise and Training

Q25. From a cultural perspective which of the following might help your company/ organisation to achieve greater success in doing business in/with China?

a) Study Chinese language   [ ]

b) Study Chinese culture   [ ]

c) Study Chinese culture and language combined   [ ]

d) Study Chinese business culture   [ ]

e) Ad hoc research services   [ ]

f) Employ university graduates specialised in Chinese studies   [ ]

g) Other (please specify) _____

Q26. What is a good way for you or your employees to acquire the training/skills listed in Q25 above?

a) Evening courses in Chinese-related studies   [ ]

b) Intensive short-term courses (3 days, 5 days, 10 days, etc.)   [ ]

c) Online distance learning   [ ]

d) Part-time degree in Chinese language and culture   [ ]

e) Study tour of China   [ ]

f) Chinese-focused MBA programme   [ ]

g) Chinese-focused MBA programme with summer tour in China [ ]

h) Other (please specify) _____

Q27. What kind of information is essential for doing business in China?

a) About Chinese culture and customs   [ ]

b) About Chinese business practices   [ ]

c) About Chinese government policies   [ ]

d) About the Chinese legal system and business law   [ ]

e) Information to help establish personal connections   [ ]

f) Other (please specify) _____

Q28. What kinds of university graduates do you think would be suitable to help your company/organisation to develop business links with China?

Name of Degree Programme	Select
a) Bachelor of Commerce (Business and Chinese Studies)	[ ]
b) Bachelor of Arts in Chinese Studies	[ ]
c) Bachelor of Arts in Politics and Chinese Studies	[ ]
d) Bachelor of Civil Law (Law and Chinese Studies)	[ ]

Name of Degree Programme	Select
e) Bachelor of Arts in Chinese Studies and French	[ ]
f) Bachelor of Arts in Chinese Studies and German	[ ]
g) Bachelor of Arts in History and Chinese Studies	[ ]
h) Bachelor of Arts in Music and Chinese Studies	[ ]
i) Master of Arts in Contemporary China Studies	[ ]
j) Master of Science in Chinese Business Studies	[ ]
k) Other (please specify) _____	

Q29. If you have more suggestions about how we can help your company/organisation achieve greater success in doing business in/with China, please write them below:

....

....

Part Six: Summary Report

Please indicate if you would like to have a copy of our summary report. (Your response to this questionnaire will remain anonymous and confidential.)

Yes, by email [   ] (Please give name and email address) _____

Yes, by mail   [   ] (Please give name and address) _____

No thank you [   ]

Thank you very much for your support and cooperation.

Appendix B

Methodology

RESEARCH DESIGN

The initial objective of this research was to investigate the demand amongst Irish companies and organisations for Chinese expertise, and also for training in Chinese language and culture. To this end, the cultural issues which had played a role in Irish companies and organisations doing business in or with China were included in the investigation. An initial preliminary survey was conducted, which involved the distribution of a pilot questionnaire to a small group of Irish businesspeople; this was followed by a literature search to help analyse the data collected from the survey.

Based on the preliminary research, a new questionnaire was designed in which the important cultural issues that were revealed in the preliminary research were added, including the differences and similarities between Irish and Chinese culture and intercultural trust issues between Irish businesspeople and their Chinese partners and employees.

QUESTIONNAIRE SURVEY

The major questionnaire survey was conducted among the members of Ireland China Association (ICA), as a majority of Irish businesspeople doing business in or with China belong to this organisation. In total, 365 questionnaires were posted out to the members of the association and 77 were returned, a high response rate of 21.1 per cent.

The questionnaire was also distributed to the members of the Irish Exporters Association. One difference between this and the ICA is that their members are involved in the import and export business generally throughout Asia and beyond, rather than in China alone. As a result, a lower response rate was received: in total 110 questionnaires were posted out and 15 were returned, a response rate of 13.6 per cent.

The members of the trade mission to China in 2005 and in 2008 were also surveyed. Ninety-eight questionnaires were posted out according to a name list published by Enterprise Ireland and seven questionnaires were returned, a response rate of 7.1 per cent. Some questionnaires were returned indicating that the people were no longer at the addresses to which the questionnaires were posted. This may have contributed to the relatively lower response rate from this group.

In addition, an electronic version of the questionnaire was used to survey a much wider range of people, including members of the Marketing Institute of Ireland and Alumni of UCD Business School, both of which included a link to the survey on Survey Monkey* in their electronic newsletter. Membership of these two organisations numbered 6,000 and 1,300 respectively, but would have had relatively few people involved in doing business in or with China. Ten questionnaires were received from these two groups; the exact response rate from these is not given, as the numbers who visited the websites during the period the questionnaire survey was conducted remains unknown.

The remaining eight returned questionnaires were completed by Irish businesspeople who did not belong to any of the above organisations but who had either participated in our interview survey or had been contacted through Irish social networks in China.

DATA ANALYSIS

The quantitative data generated from the questionnaire survey was summarised using tables and diagrams. Cross-tabulations (crosstab) were used to examine the interdependence between two or more variables. By displaying the joint distribution of two or more variables in a matrix format, the crosstabs showed specific data values and provided more implicit information. The method also helped us compare the frequency of occurrences of categories or values. In this case, multiple bar charts were applied to reveal differences, while stacked bar charts were applied to show totals.

---

* An internet-based service that allows surveys and questionnaires to be submitted online.

INTERVIEWS

A brief initial analysis of the returned questionnaires and four pilot interviews facilitated the design of a semi-structured interview schedule which would enable the further exploration of some of the themes highlighted in the responses. Broadly speaking, the interviews were carried out with reference to the topics outlined in the questionnaire. Open-ended questions were utilised to ensure that responses were grounded and emerged from informants' own perspectives.

The interviews were conducted by the research team members, each with their own interview style. Researchers were free to pursue interesting themes and revealing case histories in an effort to obtain in-depth information and allow interviewees to discuss their own particular experiences and concerns. The quotations from the interviews have a code identifier indicating the interviewer and the interview number.

In order to obtain information in a way that covered the diversity of the context, interviewees were selected from as wide a range of occupations and sectors to provide as good a cross-section as possible. In total, 28 Irish people were interviewed. All had connections to business in China. Each interview lasted about one and a half hours, and most were recorded by audio device (26). Two interviews were recorded by means of written notes. Transcriptions were made and then sorted by topic.

PILOT TRAINING PROGRAMMES

Owing to the overwhelming demand for business training in Chinese culture and language expressed by the Irish businesspeople in response to the questionnaire and in interviews, it was decided that pilot programmes would be run for Irish businesspeople at both senior and junior executive levels between May and July 2009.

On 7 May 2009, the UCD Confucius Institute for Ireland, partnered by the Ireland China Association, delivered a one-day bespoke training programme on Chinese business and culture for senior executives from CRH Group, the Irish Fortune 500 multinational building materials and construction services company whose global operations include major investment in China.

Furthermore, from 21 April to 7 July 2009, the UCD Confucius Institute for Ireland, partnered by the Ireland China Association, delivered a twelve-week course in Chinese language, business and culture, which was attended by members of business organisations, the civil service and the public.

The two pilot training programmes received overwhelmingly positive responses from participants. Case studies of the two programmes are incorporated here, from which a great deal can be learned about the potential of such programmes.

Appendix C

Executive Summary

The findings of the survey are summarised as follows:

- Four out of every five respondents intend to increase their business dealings in China in the next five years and the majority of them have had more than three years' experience in the Chinese market.
- Almost all respondents emphasised the importance of an awareness of cultural factors for successful business dealings in China. However, less than two in five respondents had participated in training in language, culture or doing business in China.
- Respondents emphasised the substantial differences between Irish and Chinese business culture and environments and the cultural issues associated with developing human relationships in business. The vast majority, 84.3 per cent, of respondents indicated that good personal relationships was the most important key factor in achieving greater success in the Chinese market, and 88 per cent that information about Chinese business practices is essential for doing business in China.
- Understanding the Chinese market was identified by 67.8 per cent as one of the top three sociocultural factors that can contribute to business success in China. On the other hand, aspects of the Chinese market such as Chinese government policies, regulations, the legal system and business law had caused tremendous challenges for Irish companies and organisations. More than two out of five expressed their concerns about dealing with Chinese regulations, and about one-third about government policies.
- Some respondents felt that Irish businesspeople have an advantage compared to other Europeans and Americans in adapting to the Chinese market due to certain similarities between Irish and Chinese culture and history. Nearly half of respondents agreed

that Chinese culture shares more similarities with Irish culture than it does with other European or American cultures. Four aspects that relate to human relations were seen as 'very similar' by a significant percentage: 'do business through personal connections' (56.8 per cent), 'use long-term relationships to establish mutual trust' (48.2 per cent), 'highly values friendship' (46.8 per cent) and 'focus on family values' (45.9 per cent).

- Endeavouring to overcome cultural differences was seen as important for achieving Irish–Chinese business success. Key cultural differences where 'little similarity' was identified between both cultures were 'importance of saving face/avoiding losing face' (53.6 per cent of respondents), 'respects/obeys authority' (36.1 per cent) and 'flexible in following regulations' (34.3 per cent).

- Building mutual trust between Irish and Chinese business was recognised as requiring a consistent long-term effort covering a wide range of factors. Cross-cultural knowledge and awareness was seen as the most important factor by 61.4 per cent of respondents, given how different the Chinese political, social and economic system is. Over half considered professional competence, fulfilling promises, language abilities and personal connections as also important.

- Access to information sources was identified by more than half of the respondents as another important factor in doing business in or with China. However, among the respondents who claimed that information scarcity was a problem preventing them from achieving greater success in the Chinese market, more than half of them had no physical presence in China.

- Those having a physical business presence appeared to appreciate how essential human relations are in the Chinese business environment. As many as 93 per cent of survey respondents with a physical presence in China indicated that 'good personal relationships' have contributed or will contribute to their business success, compared with 75 per cent of those with no physical presence.

- The substantial and fast-growing commercial links between Ireland and China have led to increasing demand for tailored short training courses in the Chinese language, Chinese culture and doing business in China. Respondents had a wide range of course preferences, including intensive short-term courses (52 per cent), evening courses in Chinese-related studies (40.2 per cent), part-time degrees in Chinese language and culture (27.5 per cent), study tours of China (25.5 per cent), online distance learning (24.5 per cent) and a Chinese-focused MBA programme with a summer tour in China (21.6 per cent).

- Respondents indicated that there is a high demand in Irish companies and organisations for university-level graduates who combine Business with Chinese studies, i.e. Bachelor of Commerce with Chinese Studies (78.4 per cent). Others were Master of Science in Chinese Business Studies (48.5 per cent), Bachelor of Arts in Chinese Studies (16.5 per cent), Master of Arts in Contemporary China Studies (14.4 per cent), Bachelor of Civil Law and Chinese Studies (12.4 per cent), and Bachelor of Arts in Politics and Chinese Studies (10.3 per cent).

Chart 1: How do you perceive your business involvement in China in the next five years?

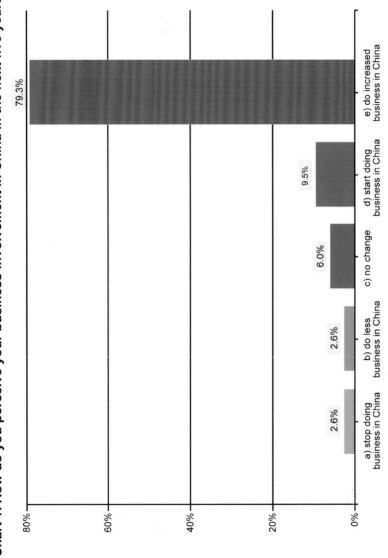

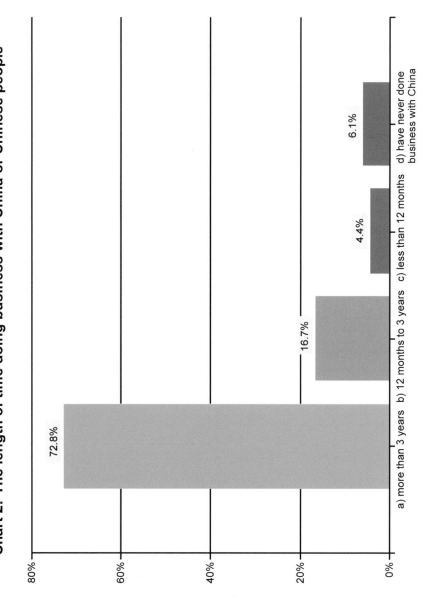

Chart 2: The length of time doing business with China or Chinese people

72.8%

16.7%

4.4%

6.1%

80% 60% 40% 20% 0%

a) more than 3 years b) 12 months to 3 years c) less than 12 months d) have never done business with China

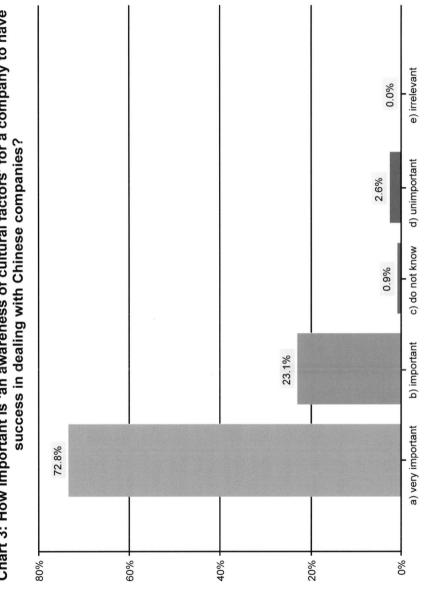

Chart 3: How important is 'an awareness of cultural factors' for a company to have success in dealing with Chinese companies?

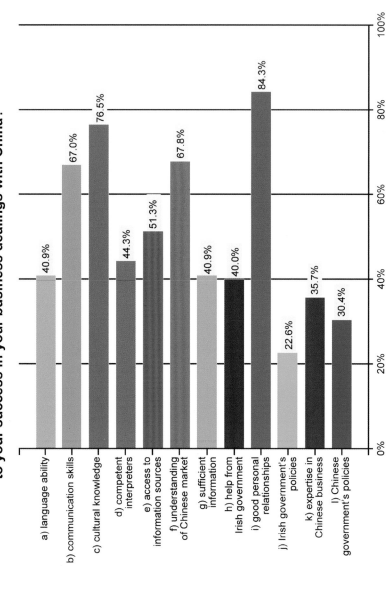

Chart 4: Which of the following factors do you think have contributed/will contribute to your success in your business dealings with China?

Factor	Percentage
a) language ability	40.9%
b) communication skills	67.0%
c) cultural knowledge	76.5%
d) competent interpreters	44.3%
e) access to information sources	51.3%
f) understanding of Chinese market	67.8%
g) sufficient information	40.9%
h) help from Irish government	40.0%
i) good personal relationships	84.3%
j) Irish government's policies	22.6%
k) expertise in Chinese business	35.7%
l) Chinese government's policies	30.4%

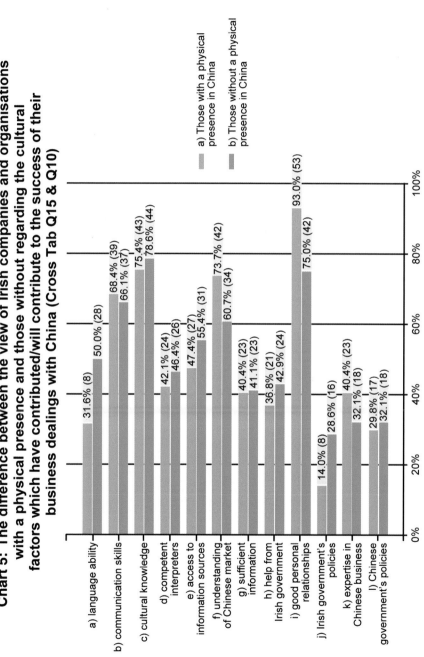

Chart 5: The difference between the view of Irish companies and organisations with a physical presence and those without regarding the cultural factors which have contributed/will contribute to the success of their business dealings with China (Cross Tab Q15 & Q10)

a) Those with a physical presence in China

b) Those without a physical presence in China

a) language ability — 31.6% (8), 50.0% (28)
b) communication skills — 68.4% (39), 66.1% (37)
c) cultural knowledge — 75.4% (43), 78.6% (44)
d) competent interpreters — 42.1% (24), 46.4% (26)
e) access to information sources — 47.4% (27), 55.4% (31)
f) understanding of Chinese market — 73.7% (42), 60.7% (34)
g) sufficient information — 40.4% (23), 41.1% (23)
h) help from Irish government — 36.8% (21), 42.9% (24)
i) good personal relationships — 93.0% (53), 75.0% (42)
j) Irish government's policies — 14.0% (8), 28.6% (16)
k) expertise in Chinese business — 40.4% (23), 32.1% (18)
l) Chinese government's policies — 29.8% (17), 32.1% (18)

Chart 6: The diference between Irish companies and organisations with a physical presence and those without regarding the problems which are preventing them from achieving greater success in doing business in/with China (Cross Tab Q21 & Q10)

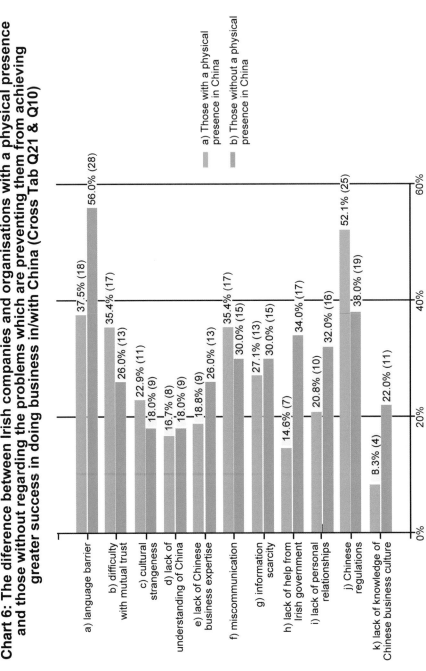

Chart 7: Do you think Chinese culture shares more similarities with Irish culture than it does with other European cultures or with American culture?

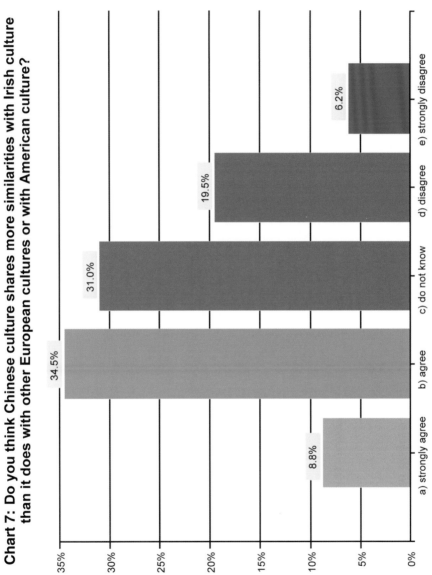

Chart 8: In the case of each of the following, please rank what you consider to be the degree of similarity between Irish and Chinese cultures

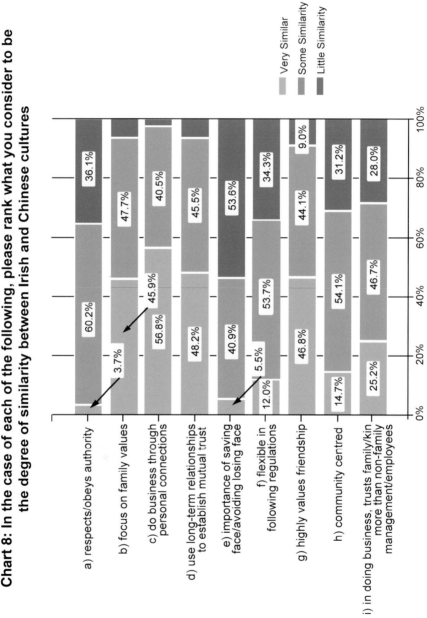

Legend:
- Very Similar
- Some Similarity
- Little Similarity

Categories:
- a) respects/obeys authority — 60.2%, 36.1%
- b) focus on family values — 3.7%, 47.7%
- c) do business through personal connections — 56.8%, 45.9%, 40.5%
- d) use long-term relationships to establish mutual trust — 48.2%, 45.5%
- e) importance of saving face/avoiding losing face — 40.9%, 53.6%
- f) flexible in following regulations — 12.0%, 5.5%, 53.7%, 34.3%
- g) highly values friendship — 46.8%, 44.1%, 9.0%
- h) community centred — 14.7%, 54.1%, 31.2%
- i) in doing business, trusts family/kin more than non-family management/employees — 25.2%, 46.7%, 28.0%

Chart 9: In your opinion, how important is intercultural trust for successfully doing business in or with China?

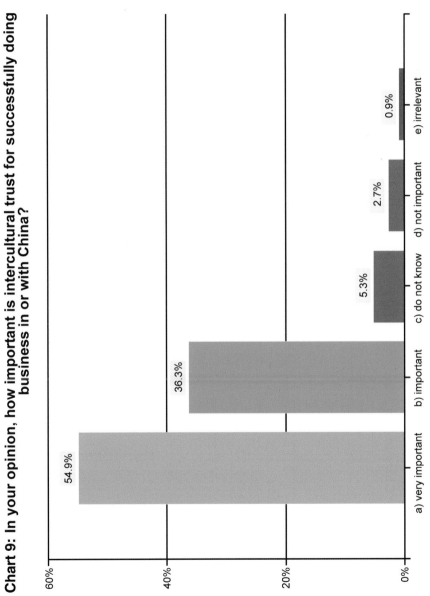

Chart 10: In your opinion, which of the following factors would contribute to building successful mutual trust between your company/organisation and your Chinese business partner(s) and/or your Chinese employees?

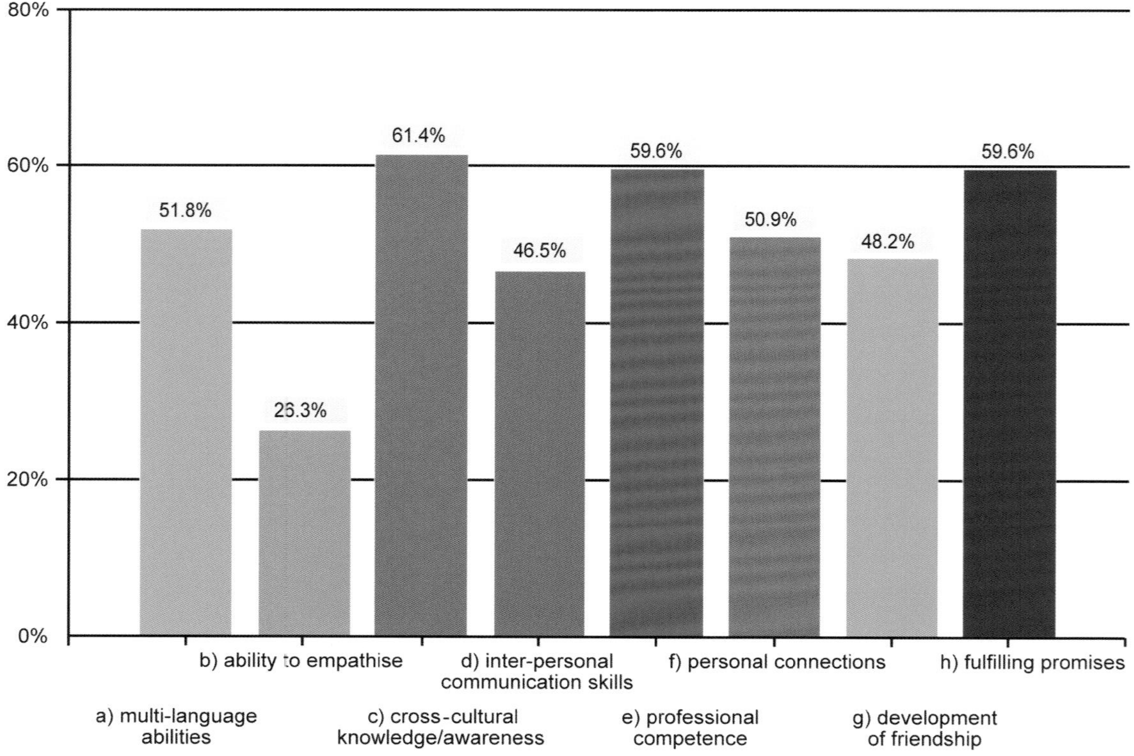

Factor	Percentage
a) multi-language abilities	51.8%
b) ability to empathise	26.3%
c) cross-cultural knowledge/awareness	61.4%
d) inter-personal communication skills	46.5%
e) professional competence	59.6%
f) personal connections	50.9%
g) development of friendship	48.2%
h) fulfilling promises	59.6%

Chart 11: Which of the following problems are preventing you from achieving greater success in doing business in or with China?

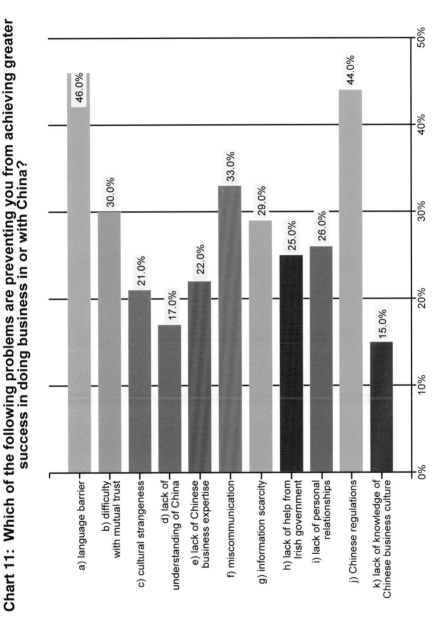

Chart 12: Please rank, in order, the three most important factors from those you have listed in Q21

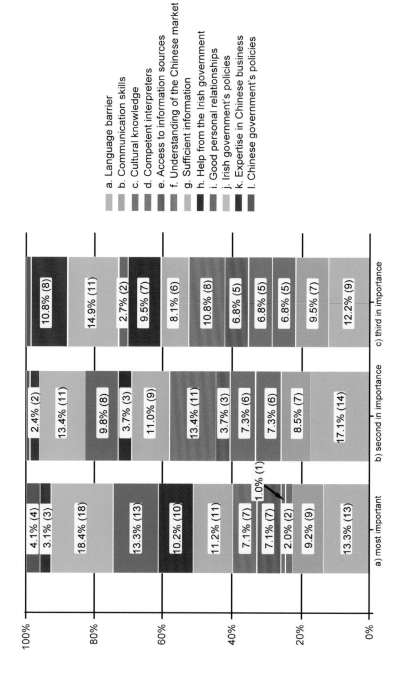

a. Language barrier
b. Communication skills
c. Cultural knowledge
d. Competent interpreters
e. Access to information sources
f. Understanding of the Chinese market
g. Sufficient information
h. Help from the Irish government
i. Good personal relationships
j. Irish government's policies
k. Expertise in Chinese business
l. Chinese government's policies

Chart 13: What kind of information is essential for doing business in China?

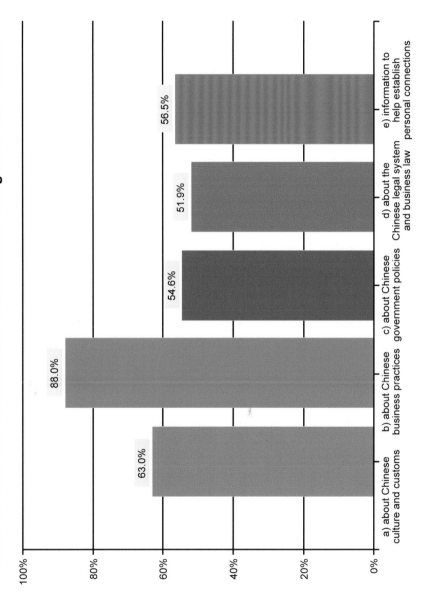

Chart 14: What kinds of university graduates do you think would be suitable to help your company/organisation to develop business links with China?

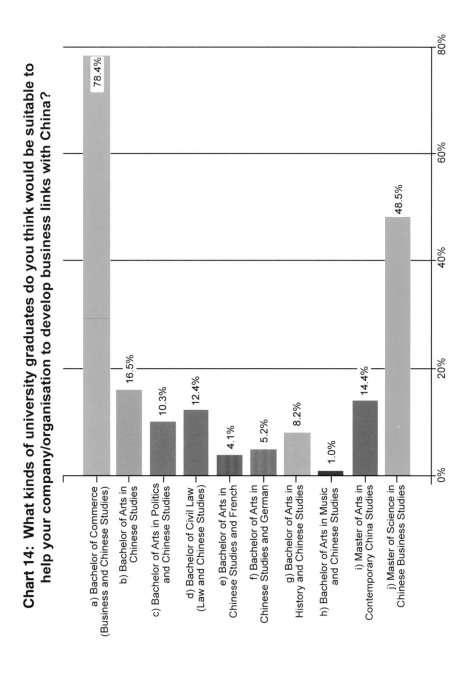

Chart 15: What is a good way for you or your employees to acquire training/skills in Chinese language, culture and business culture?

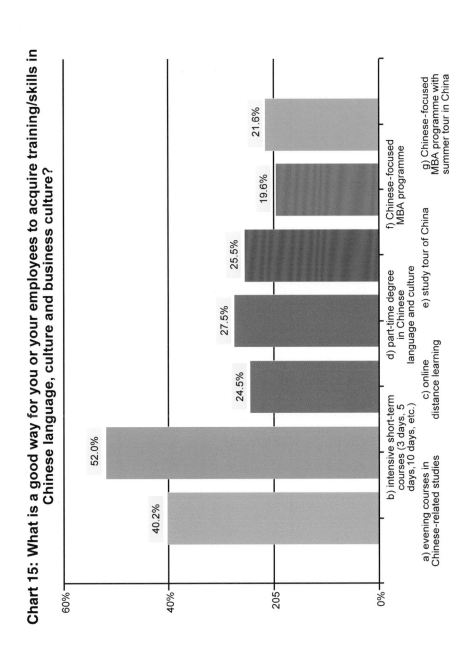

a) evening courses in Chinese-related studies — 40.2%
b) intensive short-term courses (3 days, 5 days,10 days, etc.) — 52.0%
c) online distance learning — 24.5%
d) part-time degree in Chinese language and culture — 27.5%
e) study tour of China — 25.5%
f) Chinese-focused MBA programme — 19.6%
g) Chinese-focused MBA programme with summer tour in China — 21.6%

Chart 16: From a cultural perspective which of the following might help your company/organisation to achieve greater success in doing business in or with China?

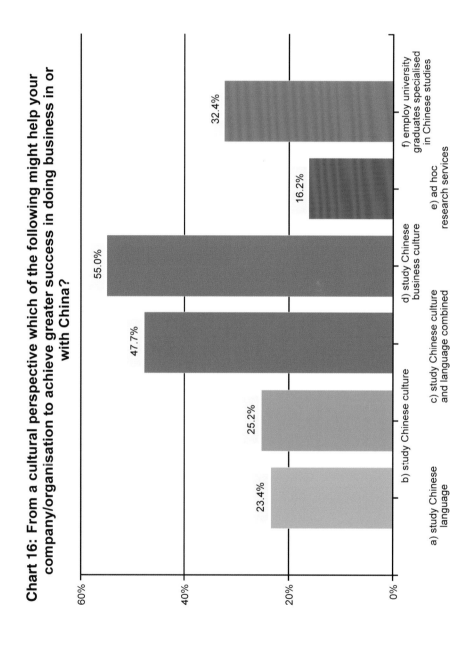